DIABETIC DIET AFTER 60 COOKBOOK

Live Well, Eat Better: Simple Low-Carb Recipes to Improve Health, Designed for Life After 60

Jonny Bakers

© Copyright 2024 by Jonny Bakers - All rights reserved.

The following book is provided below with the aim of delivering information that is as precise and dependable as possible. However, purchasing this book implies an acknowledgment that both the publisher and the author are not experts in the discussed topics, and any recommendations or suggestions contained herein are solely for entertainment purposes. It is advised that professionals be consulted as needed before acting on any endorsed actions.

This statement is considered fair and valid by both the American Bar Association and the Committee of Publishers Association, and it holds legal binding throughout the United States.

Moreover, any transmission, duplication, or reproduction of this work, including specific information, will be deemed an illegal act, regardless of whether it is done electronically or in print. This includes creating secondary or tertiary copies of the work or recorded copies, which are only allowed with the express written consent from the Publisher. All additional rights are reserved.

The information in the following pages is generally considered to be a truthful and accurate account of facts. As such, any negligence, use, or misuse of the information by the reader will result in actions falling solely under their responsibility. There are no scenarios in which the publisher or the original author can be held liable for any difficulties or damages that may occur after undertaking the information described herein.

Additionally, the information in the following pages is intended solely for informational purposes and should be considered as such. As fitting its nature, it is presented without assurance regarding its prolonged validity or interim quality. Mention of trademarks is done without written consent and should not be construed as an endorsement from the trademark holder.

TABLE OF CONTENTS

INTRODUCTION 9
1. THE IMPORTANCE OF DIET IN AGING 9
2. HOW DIABETES AFFECTS OLDER ADULTS 12
3. USING THIS COOKBOOK FOR OPTIMAL HEALTH 15
4. LIFESTYLE CHANGES FOR BETTER DIABETES MANAGEMENT 17

DIABETES AFTER 60 21
1. UNDERSTANDING DIABETES TYPES AND RISKS 21
2. SYMPTOMS AND EARLY WARNING SIGNS 24
3. DIABETES COMPLICATIONS IN SENIORS 26
4. STRATEGIES FOR LONG-TERM HEALTH 28

MANAGE DIABETES: 31
1. BUILDING A SUSTAINABLE MEAL PLAN 31
2. SMART SNACKING FOR BLOOD SUGAR CONTROL 34
3. TIPS FOR DINING OUT 37
4. MONITORING AND ADAPTING TO BLOOD SUGAR CHANGES 40

MACRONUTRIENTS AND MICRONUTRIENTS 45
1. THE ROLE OF CARBOHYDRATES AND FIBER 45
2. CHOOSING HEALTHY FATS 47
3. PROTEINS FOR MUSCLE MAINTENANCE 49
4. ESSENTIAL VITAMINS AND MINERALS FOR DIABETES 51

BREAKFAST 55
1. LOW-CARB MORNING STAPLES 55
    Spinach and Feta Breakfast Scramble 55
    Smoked Salmon and Avocado Salad 56
    Cauliflower Hash Browns 57
    Greek Yogurt and Berry Parfait 58
    Tofu and Vegetable Stir-Fry 58
2. SWEET YET SUGAR-FREE MORNINGS 60

Cinnamon Apple Chia Pudding 60

Berry Yoghurt Smoothie Bowl 61

Fluffy Cottage Cheese Pancakes 62

Spinach and Mushroom Omelette 63

Grapefruit and Avocado Salad 64

LUNCH 67

1. Power Salads and Bowls 67

Mediterranean Tuna and Bean Salad 67

Spicy Shrimp and Avocado Salad 68

2. Hearty Yet Healthy Mains 70

Zesty Lemon Herb Grilled Salmon 70

DINNER 73

1. Comfort Foods, Diabetic Style 73

Diabetic-Friendly Stuffed Bell Peppers 73

Lemon Herb Baked Salmon 74

Creamy Tomato and Spinach Pasta 75

2. Light Yet Satisfying Evening Meals 77

Zesty Lime and Herb Grilled Salmon 77

Mediterranean Stuffed Bell Peppers 78

Ginger Soy Tofu Stir-Fry 79

FREE SUGAR DESSERT 81

1. Naturally Sweetened Treats 81

Almond & Berry Breakfast Tart 81

Cinnamon Spice Poached Pears 82

Chocolate Avocado Mousse 83

Lemon & Chia Seed Pudding 83

2. Fruit-Based Delights 85

Berry Bliss Parfait 85

Citrus Mint Melon Balls 86

No-Bake Cherry Delight 87

Pear Ginger Clusters 88

SNACKS AND SIDES 91

1. Savory Snacks for Steady Blood Sugar 91

Smoked Salmon and Avocado Roll-Ups 91

Chickpea and Spinach Stuffed Portobellos 92

2. Guilt-Free Sides for Every Meal 94

Zesty Lemon Asparagus 94

Refreshing Cucumber-Mint Salad 95

Savory Roasted Green Beans 96

30 DAYS MEAL PLAN 99

MEASUREMENT CONVERSION TABLE 105

CONCLUSION 109

THANK YOU FROM THE BOTTOM OF MY HEART 112

INTRODUCTION

1. THE IMPORTANCE OF DIET IN AGING

As we gracefully age into our sixties and beyond, each passing year adds depth to our perspective, wisdom to our encounters, and, inevitably, challenges to our health. Among these challenges, managing dietary habits emerges as a pivotal concern, especially for those living with diabetes. It's no secret that our dietary needs shift as we age, but understanding exactly how and why these changes matter can make an undeniable difference in our quality of life.

The significance of diet in aging transcends mere calorie counting or avoiding certain foods. It encompasses a foundational shift in how we perceive and interact with our nourishment. After all, our diet is not just what we eat; it's a crucial tool for sculpting our health, maintaining independence, and maximizing our vitality during the golden years.

Aging brings about various physiological changes that affect metabolism, nutrient absorption, and even taste preferences. For example, our digestive system becomes less efficient with age, impacting how well nutrients are extracted from the food we consume. Similarly, changes in taste may lead the palette to favor sweeter or saltier foods, which can be detrimental if not managed wisely.

For those navigating life with diabetes, these natural shifts underline the importance of a carefully considered diet. It's not just about managing blood sugar levels, although that is certainly a priority. It's also about preventing or managing other age-related conditions, like heart disease, bone density loss, and muscle atrophy, which can be exacerbated by diabetes.

To put this into perspective, let's consider carbohydrates — a hot topic for anyone with diabetes. In our youth, carbs are often seen as energy sources, fueling everything from brain function to physical activity. As we age, and particularly for those managing diabetes, carbohydrates can become a double-edged sword. The type, quantity, and timing of carbohydrate intake must be handled with precision to prevent adverse effects on blood sugar levels while still ensuring sufficient energy and nutritional intake. Here's where the broader picture of dietary importance in aging comes into play. A diet rich in fiber, for instance, becomes increasingly significant.

Fiber aids digestion, helps regulate blood sugar levels, and can impact cholesterol levels, which is crucial as heart health becomes more fragile in our senior years. But the story doesn't end with fiber.

Antioxidants found in fruits and vegetables become heroes in this chapter of life, fighting against cellular damage and inflammation, and potentially warding off diseases like Alzheimer's and certain cancers. Then there are proteins – essential for maintaining muscle mass, which naturally declines with age. Adequate protein intake supports strength, mobility, and overall vitality.

But how does one manage to balance all these needs, particularly with the shadow of diabetes looming overhead? It starts with understanding that no single diet fits all. Tailoring your diet to fit your metabolic state, activity level, and medical needs is imperative. The approach one might take is not about imposing strict limitations but rather about embracing moderation and making wise choices.

For instance, introducing more whole foods and reducing reliance on processed items can greatly enhance the nutritional quality of your diet. Foods that are close to their natural state are not only packed with necessary vitamins and minerals but also free of unnecessary additives and high in fiber.

Moreover, hydration plays a role that cannot be overstressed. With age, our sense of thirst diminishes, which can lead to dehydration, affecting everything from cognitive function to kidney health. Remember, water is crucial in processing nutrients and medications efficiently.

Another aspect worth considering is meal timing and frequency. As metabolism slows, the traditional three large meals a day may no longer suit your body's needs. Many find that smaller, more frequent meals can help maintain energy levels throughout the day and keep blood sugar levels more stable.

In addressing these dietary factors, we not only manage diabetes more effectively but also enhance our ability to enjoy our later years. Imagine being able to play with your grandchildren in the park, travel, or engage in community activities without the constant worry about sudden blood sugar spikes or feeling fatigued due to poor dietary choices. This optimized approach to diet in our advanced years is not about restriction but about transformation. It's a commitment to celebrate life with every nutritious meal you choose. As we understand and respect our aging bodies, we pave the way for a senior life marked not just by years, but by life quality. In crafting your journey through the twilight years with diabetes, recall that change is the only constant, and adaptation is your greatest ally. By choosing to manage your diet, you're not just controlling diabetes; you're embracing a pathway to preserve your zest for life, ensuring that each meal nourishes not just the body, but also the soul. Through mindful eating, we can address the physical changes that age introduces, combating diabetes with dignity, and perhaps most importantly, with pleasure.

2. How Diabetes Affects Older Adults

Navigating the golden years requires not just a map of where you've been, but a clear understanding of the changes the body undergoes, which influence every aspect of life. For older adults, who often contend with multiple health matters, diabetes stands out as particularly impactful. It quietly redefines what aging looks like, feels like, and, significantly, how it can be managed.

Diabetes in older adults isn't merely a continuation of the diabetes known at younger ages; it presents uniquely, complicates other health conditions, and demands specialized understanding and care. As we delve into this terrain, let's illuminate how diabetes reshapes the health landscape for seniors, inviting not just challenges but opportunities for greater awareness and care that can enhance the later chapters of one's life.

Firstly, it's imperative to recognize that the human body at 60, 70, or beyond, doesn't process glucose the same way it once did. Age-related insulin resistance and impaired pancreatic function mean that blood sugar management becomes a delicate balance. The stakes are high, as uncontrolled diabetes can accelerate the natural cognitive decline associated with aging, making day-to-day activities and memory retention harder to maintain.

Now, consider the broader medical landscape of an older adult. It's often crowded, marked by the presence of heart disease, hypertension, deteriorating vision, and reduced kidney function. Diabetes interacts with these conditions in ways that can compound their effects. For instance, the disease's impact on blood vessels can exacerbate heart conditions or lead to diabetic retinopathy, a significant cause of vision loss in the aging population.

The kidneys, too, tell a part of this story. They work tirelessly to filter the blood, a job made harder by diabetes, which can lead to kidney disease or exacerbate existing impairment. As kidney function declines, the implications ripple outward, affecting everything from medication choices to the body's ability to stay hydrated.

Moreover, the threat of hypoglycemia—or dangerously low blood sugar—looms larger as we age. The usual warnings signs of hypoglycemia, like shakiness or sweating, might be less noticeable or attributed to other health issues common in older adults. Thus, managing diabetes is not just about preventing high blood sugar levels but also ensuring they do not drop too low, a balance that requires meticulous understanding and constant vigilance.

One cannot discuss diabetes in older adults without noting the role of mobility and physical activity. With age, staying active can become challenging due to pain, joint problems, or other health issues, yet physical activity is key in managing diabetes effectively. It helps improve insulin sensitivity, reduce blood pressure, and maintain muscle mass, which all contribute to better

overall health and reduced diabetic complications. Another element to consider is the psychological impact of diabetes on older adults. Living with this condition can be isolating, particularly when it necessitates dietary restrictions or complicates social interactions and activities. The mental burden of managing a chronic condition, along with fears about complications and dependency, can lead to increased rates of depression and anxiety. This emotional aspect is crucial since mental health greatly influences physical health, especially in diabetes management.

Turning to prevention and management, the role of personalized medical care becomes central. Treatment plans for diabetes in the elderly must be tailored—what works for a 30-year-old might not be suitable for a 75-year-old. This includes adjusting dietary recommendations, exercise routines, and medications to individual capabilities, preferences, and social conditions.

The complexities of managing diabetes in older adults mean that medical consultations should extend beyond mere prescription adjustments; they should encompass discussions about diet, physical activity, mental health, and practical issues like vision and mobility, ensuring a holistic approach to care.

In this context, the value of a strong support system cannot be overstressed. Family, friends, and healthcare providers form a network that can offer not just medical but moral support. Regularly checking in, assisting with meals, encouraging gentle exercise, or simply lending an ear can make a meaningful difference in an older adult's diabetes management journey.

Indeed, managing diabetes as one ages is as much about controlling blood sugar as it is about adapting to an evolving life narrative. It requires resilience and a proactive approach to adapt strategies over time. Embracing these changes with the right knowledge can transform the management of diabetes from a daily challenge into an integral part of a fulfilling and active later life. Understanding diabetes in the context of older adulthood is not just about foreseeing problems but about equipping oneself with the knowledge to tackle them head-on. It's about turning the golden years into a period not of decline but of managed, vibrant living, where every moment is lived with dignity and independence. This nuanced approach allows those impacted by diabetes to chart a course through aging that is as healthy and enjoyable as possible, backed by a clear understanding of the intersections between diabetes and aging.

3. USING THIS COOKBOOK FOR OPTIMAL HEALTH

Imagine stepping into a kitchen where every ingredient, every stir, and every meal is a step toward better health and vitality, especially tailored for those of us embracing the senior years of life and managing diabetes. This cookbook is designed not just as a collection of recipes but as a companion in your journey toward optimal health, offering much more than just low-sugar delights. It's an invitation to rediscover the joy of cooking with the peace of mind that every dish supports your dietary needs—balancing blood sugar, enhancing energy, and nourishing the body comprehensively. As we dive deeper into how to use this cookbook for achieving optimal health, consider it a bridge between your current lifestyle and the lifestyle you aim to lead—one where diabetes management aligns seamlessly with enjoying life's flavorful moments. The recipes here are more than just "safe" for people with diabetes; they are crafted to promote overall health, from your heart to your bones, in a way that respects the nuances of aging.

Each recipe in this collection is developed keeping in mind the common hurdles that people face at this stage of life. Gone are the days of frustratingly long ingredient lists, overly complex cooking methods, or disappointing, bland diet food. Instead, the emphasis here is on simplicity, flavor, and nutritional balance, making healthy eating a practical and enjoyable part of your daily routine.

Navigating through the cookbook, you'll find sections dedicated to all aspects of a daily diet—from hearty breakfasts to nourish you at the start of the day, to light yet fulfilling dinners that promise satisfaction without heaviness. Each recipe comes with nutritional insights that explain not just the caloric or sugar content but elaborate on the benefits of key ingredients, helping you understand why certain foods are beneficial and how they aid in managing diabetes more effectively.

Part of using this cookbook effectively involves embracing flexibility. The recipes are designed to be adaptable. Whether you have dietary restrictions other than diabetes, such as gluten intolerance or lactose sensitivity, or you simply don't care for a certain herb or spice, you'll find guidelines on how to modify dishes to meet your needs and tastes without compromising on health or flavor. Moreover, this book recognizes that eating is a social event. It includes tips on how to manage your diet when dining out, celebrating holidays, or cooking for guests.

This guidance is about maintaining the joy and social connection that meals often bring. It's about making choices that fit your dietary needs without feeling isolated or overly restricted—ensuring that you can partake in every festive occasion or simple family meal with confidence and enjoyment. In addition to recipes and meal plans, this book extends into practical strategies for overall lifestyle integration. It discusses how to align your meal routine with exercise habits, sleep patterns, and medication schedules. The holistic approach ensures that the diet becomes part of a larger lifestyle adjustment that supports diabetes management from multiple angles.

Interestingly, the approach here is not just preventive but proactive. Each section equips you with the knowledge to not only follow recipes but also to understand the workings behind them—how different foods affect blood sugar, how various cooking methods can enhance or detract from nutritional value, and how meal timings can impact your overall energy and health.

This cookbook also delves into the psychological aspect of dietary changes, offering advice on how to transition into new habits without emotional stress or feeling overwhelmed. It's important to acknowledge and address the emotional journey that accompanies physical dietary changes, especially when adapting to a life with diabetes.

Ultimately, using this cookbook should feel like embarking on a path paved with supportive advice, reliable knowledge, and, most importantly, delicious meals. It is a testament to the fact that a life with dietary restrictions doesn't have to be one of deprivation. Rather, it can be a fulfilling, flavorful journey that enhances your health without giving up the pleasures of good food.

So, as you turn each page, think of it as a step toward not just managing diabetes but thriving with it. Let each recipe bring you closer to mastering the art of diabetic-friendly cooking that caters to the mature palate and contributes to a vibrant, active senior life. The aim is clear: to empower you with every dish, to make each meal a celebration of life and health, and to ensure that your golden years are truly golden.

4. Lifestyle Changes for Better Diabetes Management

Embarking on the journey of managing diabetes after 60 isn't just about adhering to a new eating plan—it's about embracing a series of lifestyle changes that enhance the overall quality of life. These changes aren't mere adjustments; they're transformative habits that foster both physical vitality and mental well-being. At the heart of this transformation is the understanding that managing diabetes goes beyond medical prescriptions. It's a holistic approach that integrates physical activity, stress management, social interactions, and regular health monitoring into the fabric of daily life.

Physical Activity: Your Powerful Ally

Regular exercise stands as a cornerstone of diabetes management, especially as we age. But here, we're not advocating for high-intensity workouts which might not be appropriate for all seniors. Instead, the focus is on consistent, moderate physical activities tailored to individual abilities and preferences. Walking, swimming, yoga, and tai chi are excellent options that maintain cardio fitness, improve muscle strength, and enhance flexibility—all crucial for managing blood sugar levels and reducing the risk of diabetic complications.

The key is regularity and enjoyment. Exercise should be a pleasurable activity, not a chore. Thus, finding an activity you love ensures that staying active becomes a natural part of your lifestyle. Moreover, by integrating these activities into your routine, you not only manage your diabetes better but also improve your mood and energy levels, which in turn makes it easier to stick with a healthy lifestyle.

Stress Reduction: The Unseen Aspect of Diabetes Management

Stress is a less obvious but significant factor in managing diabetes. High stress levels can affect blood sugar control directly by altering hormone levels and indirectly by making it harder to maintain healthy lifestyle choices. Thus, mastering stress-management techniques is essential. Mindfulness meditation, guided imagery, and deep breathing exercises are potent tools for reducing stress. These practices not only help in calming the mind but also improve the body's response to stress, which is particularly important when hormones like cortisol can influence blood sugar levels. Moreover, engaging in hobbies that relax you, whether it's gardening, painting, or listening to music, can also serve as effective stress relievers.

Community and Social Connections

A rich social life is a vital component of a healthy lifestyle, particularly in our senior years. Social interactions not only stave off feelings of loneliness and depression but can also provide motivational support for managing chronic conditions like diabetes. Joining community groups, participating in local activities, or even frequent gatherings with friends and family can keep spirits

high and foster a supportive environment where managing health becomes a shared experience. For seniors with diabetes, sharing experiences with others who face similar challenges can be incredibly reassuring. Support groups or classes for diabetics offer space to exchange tips, discuss challenges and celebrate successes with peers who understand the nuances of living with the condition. Such exchanges often provide practical strategies that might not be evident in clinical settings.

Regular Medical Check-Ups: Beyond the Routine

Routine medical check-ups provide a foundation for excellent diabetes control. These visits are crucial for monitoring the progression of the condition and adjusting treatments as necessary. However, these check-ups should be more than just routine. They offer an opportunity to discuss concerns, learn more about managing the disease, and keep abreast of new treatments or practices that might be beneficial.

An effective relationship with healthcare providers means being open about your lifestyle, challenges, and any symptoms you're experiencing. It also involves understanding your medical needs and treatment decisions, ensuring that you're an active participant in your health management.

Self-Monitoring: Tuning into Your Body's Signals

Lastly, an empowering aspect of managing diabetes is learning to self-monitor your blood sugar levels. This not only helps in making immediate adjustments to diet and activity but also assists in understanding how different foods, stresses, and activities affect your blood glucose levels. Over time, this knowledge builds a more intuitive approach to managing your condition, one that's finely tuned to your body's unique responses.

Embracing Technology

In today's digital age, technology offers additional layers of support. From apps that help track food intake and blood sugar levels to devices that monitor physical activity and heart rate, technology can simplify the management of diabetes. Leveraging these tools can provide insights that motivate and inform better health decisions.

Conclusion

Each of these lifestyle changes contributes to a holistic approach to diabetes management that's about more than just avoiding sugar or following doctor's orders. It's about crafting a life that's rich, full, and vibrant. A life in which every element—food, activity, stress relief, socializing, and medical care—works together to create not just a healthy body, but a joyful, energetic spirit able to enjoy every moment to its fullest. As you incorporate these lifestyle modifications, the path might seem daunting at first, but remember that each small change paves the way for bigger transformations. With every step, you're not just managing diabetes—you're embracing a lifestyle that improves every facet of your well-being, ensuring that these years can be some of the best years of your life.

DIABETES AFTER 60

1. Understanding Diabetes Types and Risks

Understanding diabetes—especially as it affects those of us who have celebrated more than six decades—is more than just about recognizing a list of symptoms. It's about understanding a journey; one that requires adaptation, knowledge, and support. Let's sit down together, much like old friends do, and unravel the various types of diabetes and the risks they pose as we age.

Diabetes manifests in several forms, primarily type 1, type 2, and gestational diabetes. However, our focus here concerns the most common form among seniors—type 2 diabetes. This condition emerges when your body either resists the effects of insulin—a hormone that regulates the movement of sugar into your cells—or doesn't produce enough insulin to maintain normal glucose levels.

The risk increases as we age, not merely because of accumulated life habits but also due to changes in our body composition, like decreased muscle mass and increased fat, all of which can affect how our bodies handle insulin. Another variant, often not as widely discussed, highlights the latent autoimmune diabetes in adults (LADA). It shares characteristics with both type 1 and 2 and often goes misdiagnosed or misunderstood. Those affected may not need insulin at first but can become dependent on it over time.

So, what about risks and complications? The landscape of our body changes remarkably after 60. Blood vessels start becoming less flexible, nerves might function less efficiently, and the pancreas, where insulin comes into play, might not work as vigorously as it used to. Hence, the impact of diabetes goes beyond just high sugar levels—it can affect everything, from your cardiovascular health to your eyes and kidneys.

Take, for instance, cardiovascular disease. The risk here dovetails profoundly with diabetes as high glucose levels over time can lead to blood vessel damage and arterial blockages. Similarly, neuropathy, or nerve damage, manifests in many individuals dealing with diabetes. It starts with tingling sensations in the extremities and can lead to numbness, making it easy to miss signs of cuts or sores that can escalate into serious infections due to poor blood flow, especially in the feet.

While these conditions may paint a somber picture, the silver lining is that knowledge and proactive management can make a significant difference. How? First, through early detection. Typical telltale signs include frequent urination, undue thirst, unexplained weight loss, and fatigue. Recognizing these early can lead the way to effective management strategies.

Now, moving beyond the physical realm, let's touch upon the impact diabetes can have on our lifestyle and independence—areas deeply valued by all, but perhaps, treasured even more dearly as we grow older. The very thought of managing a chronic condition like diabetes can seem daunting and can sometimes lead to emotional and psychological stress. It can stir up fears about losing one's self-sufficiency and create anxiety around maintaining social and personal activities. Here, the strategy lies not only in medical treatment but also in nurturing a supportive community—family, friends, and fellow peers who understand and share similar experiences.

Moreover, adaptation plays a crucial role. Learning about and implementing dietary adjustments isn't just about following a new set of eating rules; it's about rethinking how we relate to food. This doesn't mean giving up the joy of eating or not being able to partake in family dinners or outings. It's about making informed choices that align with maintaining stable blood glucose levels while still enjoying life's culinary pleasures.

At this point, it's essential to consider the broader spectrum of your health regimen. Effective diabetes management is complemented by regular physical activity. Whether it's walking, swimming, yoga, or any other form of exercise you enjoy, staying active improves insulin sensitivity and helps manage weight. Remember, it's not about intense workouts but maintaining a consistent level of activity that suits your age and physical capabilities.

Lastly, monitoring your health, maintaining regular check-ups with your healthcare provider, and staying informed about your condition empower you to manage diabetes effectively. Autonomy in management fosters not just better physical health but enhances mental and emotional well-being.

Diabetes after 60 isn't just a health condition; it's a pathway that requires navigating with careful, considered steps. Armed with the right knowledge and support, you can manage diabetes in a way that not only focuses on keeping blood sugar levels in check but also enriches your life with fulfillment and independence. Thus, understanding the types of diabetes and their associated risks is the first stride in a marathon worth completing, one careful step at a time.

2. Symptoms and Early Warning Signs

Living beyond sixty carries its own set of challenges and experiences. One such challenge for many is managing diabetes, a condition that stealthily creeps into lives, often without loud announcements. Recognizing early symptoms and signs as soon as they arise can be likened to spotting the first few leaves of an invasive plant in your well-curated garden: the quicker you address it, the less room it has to grow. This conversation is akin to sitting down over a cup of tea, discussing these subtle signs that your body might be whispering, urging them to be heard.

Diabetes in seniors often masquerades as other health issues or general wear and tear of aging. The early symptoms tend to be so mild that many breeze past them. However, a closer look can reveal they are the first dominoes in a chain that could affect your entire quality of life. Understanding what to look for is the first line of defense in managing, if not staving off, diabetes.

Increased thirst and frequent urination are classic symptoms that often get dismissed. Our bodies try to rid themselves of excess glucose through urine, which pulls in more water from the tissues, leading to dehydration and a seemingly unquenchable thirst. If you find yourself waking up multiple times at night or your water consumption has noticeably increased, it might be your body signaling a cry for attention.

Fatigue, another early symptom, can easily be mistaken for the general exhaustion many feel after a busy day. But when rest doesn't seem to recharge your batteries like it used to, it's worthwhile to consider that your body's cells might not be getting the energy they need from glucose due to diabetes. This type of tiredness can cloak itself as a part of aging, making it easy to overlook as a warning sign of a deeper issue.

Unexpected weight loss can be concerning at any age, but in seniors, it should ring louder alarm bells, especially if it occurs without changes in diet or activity level. When insulin is not effectively doing its job, the body starts burning fat and muscle for energy, resulting in weight loss. While some may initially view weight loss as a silver lining, it's a serious warning against underlying problems.

Vision changes, such as sudden blurriness, should never be ignored. High blood sugar causes fluid levels in the body to shift, including in the eyes, leading to changes in one's ability to see. This symptom, in particular, can fluctuate; vision may normalize as blood sugar levels waiver, leading to confusing signals about the urgency and severity of the situation.

Infections, cuts, or sores that do not heal as quickly as before are subtle yet critical markers. High blood sugar compromises the body's ability to heal and fend off infections, turning minor abrasions into potential gateways for more severe complications. A tingling sensation or numbness in hands or feet, known as neuropathy, can start off mild and become quite severe. Often, this can be one of the earliest signs of diabetes where high blood sugar levels damage the nerves. This numbness can increase the risk of injury, as decreased sensation can decrease awareness of wounds, leading to an escalated risk of infection.

Now, while these symptoms are indicators begging for attention, they also serve as a prompt to maintain an ongoing dialogue with your healthcare providers. Regular health checkups can catch these symptoms early, leading to discussions and tests that confirm a diagnosis. The key here is not just in identifying but in responding with appropriate lifestyle adjustments—the kind one integrates mindfully.

Embracing these changes doesn't have to be daunting. It involves understanding your body's new needs and addressing them through simple, yet effective modifications in diet, exercise, and, perhaps, medications. It's like learning a new dance step; initially challenging but ultimately rhythmic and rewarding.

The narrative doesn't end once you notice these symptoms; rather, it begins a new chapter of self-awareness and care. Cultivating a lifestyle that accommodates your body's needs can transform the management of diabetes from a fearful concept to a lived experience marked by empowerment and proactive engagement.

Thus, weaving these symptoms into the fabric of your observations can help you lead a more controlled and joyful life, even with diabetes. It's about catching the whispers before they become shouts and addressing them with the wisdom and the tranquility that the years have offered you. This proactive dialogue with your own health is not just about managing diabetes—it's about embracing a fuller, more vibrant lifestyle that respects your body's changing narratives.

3. Diabetes Complications in Seniors

As the gentle waves of age lap against the shores of our lives, the vessel that is our body navigates through various health challenges—diabetes being a particularly notorious captain steering some of these changes. The journey becomes notably complex when undiagnosed or improperly managed diabetes brings aboard unwanted complications, especially in the golden years.

Risk does not come unannounced; it builds silently but surely, impacting more than just glucose levels. Understanding the significant long-term complications of diabetes is crucial. It's not about instilling fear, but fostering awareness and preparedness—it's akin to knowing the weather conditions before setting sail.

One of the most critical systems affected by prolonged high blood sugar levels is the cardiovascular system. Diabetes dramatically increases the risk of various cardiovascular problems, including coronary artery disease with chest pain (angina), heart attack, stroke, and narrowing of arteries (atherosclerosis). Imagine your heart and blood vessels as the waterways your health navigates; if these waters become turbulent through damage, the journey of life can become perilously rocky.

Kidney damage, or nephropathy, is another quiet usurper of health. The kidneys, those diligent workers filtering wastes from your blood, can be damaged by diabetes, leading to their failure or chronic kidney disease. This complication is akin to the silt that gradually accumulates in riverbeds, disrupting the ecological balance and eventually leading to a choked water flow if not dredged regularly.

Diabetes can also blur life's beautiful vistas by affecting the eyes—a condition known as diabetic retinopathy. Here, the blood vessels of the retina (the back part of the eye) are damaged. This complication can lead to blurry vision, sudden darkness, and painful difficulties with light perception. It's like navigating a nightly sea without a lighthouse; everything becomes an indistinguishable blend of shadows and dangers.

Nerve damage, or neuropathy, is a common complication that approximately half of people with diabetes experience. It manifests most often as tingling, numbness, burning, or pain—first taking hold in the tips of the toes or fingers, and gradually spreading upward. Lost sensation in the feet can mean injuries go unnoticed, leading to severe infections, sometimes even requiring amputation. It's as if you are slowly losing parts of your map, making the journey unpredictable and hazardous.

Now, diabetes doesn't just touch the physical realms but sways into mental health territories. Depression rates are higher in people with diabetes, affecting quality of life, treatment adherence, and overall health. This emotional toll can make one feel like they are perpetually sailing through stormy waters without a break in the clouds. Facing these complications squarely is essential, but not so that you live in fear of every potential symptom. Instead, consider these complications as signposts—markers that guide deeper understanding and proactive health management. Managing diabetes well through diet, exercise, regular check-ups, and medication adherence doesn't just lower blood sugar; it ensures clearer navigation through older adulthood, preventing or delaying the onset of complications.

It's about setting the right course—detecting changes early, sometimes even before they fully manifest, and adjusting your management plan accordingly. For instance, keeping an eye on your feet daily can be as routine but as crucial as checking the weather before heading out. Regular visits to your doctor, like tuning into the news, keep you informed about your body's condition.

The call to action here isn't just about avoiding complications; it's about embracing a lifestyle that considers and respects these potential challenges. Incorporating gentle, daily exercise can be your anchor, stabilizing blood sugar levels and improving vascular health. Opting for a balanced, nutritious diet works like calibrating your compass—it keeps you moving in the right direction.

Remember, each person's journey with diabetes is unique; what works for one may not work for another. It requires tuning into your body's specific needs and responses—a personalized map for this voyage—with health professionals acting as your navigational crew.

In conclusion, diabetes in senior years is a formidable foe, but awareness and proper management can tame many of the risks it poses. Consider each possibility not as a definite destiny but as a warning buoy to steer around, guiding you towards healthier, more joyous golden years. Every action you take, no matter how small, is a step toward smoother seas and a safer journey.

4. STRATEGIES FOR LONG-TERM HEALTH

Navigating the waters of aging, particularly with diabetes, can be akin to embarking on a lengthy sea voyage. It requires preparation, awareness, and a commitment to long-term health strategies. Consider a sea captain setting out for a long journey. Just as they would map out the course, check the integrity of their ship, and prepare for emergencies, managing diabetes effectively after 60 demands a similar depth of preparation and foresight. It's not just about avoiding the storms but also enjoying the journey, making daily life better, not just longer.

First and foremost, maintaining an open and transparent dialogue with healthcare providers is key. Think of these professionals as your navigational aides—without their insights and guidance, it would be much harder to steer through the complexities of diabetes management. Regular check-ups allow for adjustments in your care regimen, tailored to how your body is responding over time. They're also crucial in catching any complications early, effectively acting as the radar that spots approaching storms on the horizon.

Moreover, integrating a balanced diet into daily life stands as one of the sturdiest pillars in the foundation of diabetes management. But this doesn't imply a strict regimen of bland foods or an oppressive feeling of limitation. It's about finding balance and enjoyment in nutrition—focusing on a diverse array of foods that keep blood sugar levels stable but also keep meals exciting. Fiber-rich vegetables, whole grains, lean proteins, and heart-healthy fats should regularly appear on your plate. It's similar to stocking the ship's pantry with not only essentials but also spices that make the journey enjoyable.

Physical activity, too, is a powerful tool for managing diabetes. But let's redefine what exercise looks like for someone managing diabetes after 60. It isn't about running marathons unless that's a passion. It's about consistent, moderate activities—like walking, swimming, yoga, or tai chi—that keep the body moving and blood flowing. Regular exercise helps improve insulin sensitivity and manage body weight, and importantly, it can be a source of joy and an opportunity to engage with friends and family.

Mental health, often overlooked, is as critical as physical health. Stress management strategies like meditation, practicing mindfulness, or simply dedicating time to hobbies and interests can significantly impact overall well-being. Stress has a tangible effect on glucose levels; managing stress is not just about feeling better, but also about direct impact on physical health. Ignoring mental health is akin to a ship ignoring small leaks; eventually, they can cause significant damage.

Sleep is another fundamental aspect of long-term health strategies. Poor sleep can affect everything from mood and cognitive abilities to physical health, including insulin sensitivity and appetite regulation. Ensuring you have a regular, peaceful sleep schedule is crucial—it's the time

when the body and mind repair themselves, making it an essential part of navigating health. Medication management cannot be overstated. For many, medications are a key component in managing diabetes, and taking them correctly is paramount. This might mean organizing medications in a pillbox, setting reminders, or having regular discussions with a pharmacist or doctor about how the medications are working or any side effects experienced.

Lastly, an often-neglected but essential strategy is regular monitoring of blood sugar levels. This self-monitoring can provide immediate feedback about how lifestyle choices, foods, and activities influence your health. Think of it as the compass guiding the ship, helping to make real-time navigational decisions.

Incorporating these strategies into everyday life doesn't mean drastically changing who you are; it means adapting your habits to steer towards better health outcomes. It's about making small, manageable changes that fit your lifestyle, gradually setting new courses that lead to calmer waters. Sustainable habits lead to sustainable health, allowing not just longer life but improving the quality of every additional year.

Embrace this journey with confidence, knowing each small step contributes to a broader voyage towards health and happiness. Enjoy the scenery along the way, the people who join you on the journey, and the tranquil waters you can navigate through the effective management of your diabetes. Each day is both a challenge to meet and an opportunity to live well, despite—and with—diabetes.

MANAGE DIABETES:
1. BUILDING A SUSTAINABLE MEAL PLAN

When you enter your golden years, managing diabetes requires a gentle shift in how you perceive meals and mealtimes. It's about embracing a sustainable way of eating that not only takes care of your glucose levels but also brings joy and nourishment—every single day. Building a sustainable meal plan isn't just about stacking nutrients and counting calories; it's a holistic approach designed to fit seamlessly into your lifestyle while enhancing your health.

Imagine this: You wake up each morning feeling confident about your day's meals; knowing they are all prepared to meet your nutritional needs, control your blood sugar, and above all, satisfy your palate. That sense of security is what a well-rounded meal plan offers. Let's walk through what it looks like to create one that will stick with you in the long term, adapting as your needs evolve.

Understanding the Foundation of a Diabetic Meal Plan

The cornerstone of managing diabetes, especially after crossing the threshold of sixty, hinges on understanding and balancing macronutrients—carbohydrates, proteins, and fats—in each meal. Carbohydrates have the most immediate effect on blood sugar levels. However, the goal isn't to eliminate them but to choose types that have a slower, more gradual impact on glucose levels. Whole grains, leafy greens, and other fibrous vegetables become central rather than white bread or sugary snacks.

Proteins and fats are about adding satisfaction and stability. They help smooth out blood sugar levels and keep you feeling full longer. Including a moderate portion of lean proteins like fish, chicken, and vegetarian options like lentils or chickpeas, along with healthy fats such as avocados or a sprinkle of seeds, can provide sustained energy without the spikes.

Incorporating Variety for Palate and Health

The brilliance of a sustainable meal plan shines through its variety. Eating a wide range of foods ensures that no one meal becomes boring, and it helps cover all nutritional bases—from essential vitamins to antioxidants that play a role in managing diabetes complications. Each meal is a new opportunity to explore flavors from different herbs, spices, and cuisines that perhaps you never thought you'd try after sixty. Picture yourself exploring the vibrant flavors of a Mediterranean diet one week, with its emphasis on whole grains, fruits, vegetables, and fish. The next week, you might lean into some vegetarian meals that spotlight legumes and tofu—rich in proteins yet friendly to your blood sugar. The exploration of food becomes not only a quest for health but a culinary adventure.

The Role of Consistent Eating Times

Regularity in your eating schedule plays a crucial role in stabilizing blood sugar levels. Eating your meals and snacks at similar times each day can help your body regulate insulin more efficiently. it keeps the metabolism steady, aids in better digestion, and prevents sudden drops or spikes in blood sugar.

This doesn't mean rigid hour-by-hour schedules that add stress rather than relieve it, but rather a reliable pattern that your body can get accustomed to. A relaxed breakfast every morning at around the same time, lunch, dinner, and perhaps a couple of planned snacks align your body's natural rhythms with your dietary needs.

Adjusting Portions with Aging

As we age, our metabolic rate often slows down, and our caloric needs decrease. However, nutrient density—an index measuring the amount of nutrients relative to the energy (calories) a food provides—should remain high. This means slightly smaller portions overall, but with every bite packed full of nutrients to support body functions, manage diabetes, and maintain muscle mass and bone strength.

There's an art to portion control that doesn't feel like restriction. It's about replacing some calorie-dense foods with nutrient-dense ones. Think substituting a large rice serving with a vibrant veggie stir-fry or choosing fruit over a sugary dessert. Through these adjustments, the meal remains filling but better aligned with your body's needs.

Listening to Your Body's Feedback

Adapting to how your body responds to different foods and meals is perhaps the most personalized aspect of a diabetic meal plan. Blood glucose monitoring, while often viewed as purely a medical necessity, can be an insightful feedback tool to refine your diet. Maybe a certain type of grain doesn't suit you as well, or a specific mix of foods causes energy dips. Listening and adjusting is key. Engage with your dietitian or healthcare provider about these readings. Their insights can guide tweaks in your meal plan, ensuring that it not only helps maintain optimal blood sugar levels but also adapts to your body's unique responses. Building a meal plan for life after sixty, particularly with diabetes in mind, is as much about nourishing the body as it is about enjoying the food on your plate. It's about creating a flexible, flavorful approach to eating that stands the test of time, supporting both your physical health and your joy in the everyday pleasure of eating well. This is not just a diet; it's a durable, enjoyable way of life that keeps you thriving.

2. Smart Snacking for Blood Sugar Control

In managing diabetes after the age of 60, one might undervalue the humble snack, thinking it's merely a tide-over between meals. Yet, these smaller bites can play an intriguing role in stabilizing blood sugar levels throughout the day. Snacking smart isn't just about reaching for whatever is handy in the kitchen; it's a nuanced art that ensures you maintain energy, control hunger, and keep your blood sugar in check without compromising on enjoyment or social spontaneity.

Snacking wisely often starts with a change in how we think about these between-meal sustenance's. It's not about denying yourself the pleasure of eating but choosing what aligns with your health needs and satisfies your taste buds.

The Power of Balance

Consider the story of Eleanor, a vibrant 68-year-old who loves gardening and spends her afternoons tending to her roses and herbs. After being diagnosed with type 2 diabetes, Eleanor found her energy levels waning mid-afternoon, affecting her gardening. The solution wasn't less time outdoors but finding the right snack to rekindle her energy without causing a spike in her glucose levels.

Her choice? A small handful of almonds and a few slices of apple. This combo offers a good mix of healthy fats, fiber, and a touch of sweetness, providing sustained energy while keeping her blood sugar stable. Like Eleanor, finding a go-to snack that includes a mix of macronutrients (fats, proteins, and carbohydrates) can prevent the rapid rises and falls in blood sugar that lead to energy slumps.

Timing Is Everything

There's also an art to timing. Snacking isn't a sporadic grab-for-food when the mood strikes; it's a strategically timed mini-meal. For instance, integrating a mid-morning and mid-afternoon snack into your routine can be more effective than the traditional three large meals a day. This approach can curb excessive hunger at mealtimes, which often leads to overeating and subsequent glucose spikes.

But how do you pick the perfect time? Listen to your body—it's the best indicator. Regular monitoring of your blood sugar will help you understand how different foods and timing affect your levels. This biofeedback is invaluable in crafting a snacking schedule that harmonizes with your body's natural rhythms.

Smart Choices Over Easy Choices

In the world of instant gratification, it's easy to fall prey to the convenience of packaged snacks—often laden with hidden sugars and unhealthy fats. Instead, the key is preparing ahead. Let's take Tom, a 72-year-old book enthusiast who enjoys reading through the afternoons. Tom prepares small containers of mixed nuts and seeds at the start of each week. Whenever he sits down with a book, he always has a container within arm's reach—a much better choice than the high-sugar granola bars he used to snack on.

Preparing these snacks ahead of time means you always have a healthy option at your fingertips, reducing the temptation to indulge in less healthy alternatives. It's not about avoiding snacking; it's about being prepared with better options.

The Social Dimension of Snacking

Managing diabetes shouldn't isolate you from enjoyable social interactions. Think about the gatherings, the family meet-ups, the Sunday brunches—occasions where often, snacks, rather than full meals, are shared. For those of us intent on maintaining stable blood sugar levels, it does require a bit of planning ahead.

Bringing a diabetes-friendly dish to share not only ensures you have a healthy option available, but it also introduces your family and friends to the tasty, nutritious possibilities that your diet includes. It can be a delightful way to educate those you love about your choices and encourage them to consider their own dietary habits.

Continuous Adaptation

Lastly, a word on evolving needs. As your body changes, so does its response to foods. What works well at 60 might need adjustment by 65. In addition to regular discussions with your dietitian, keeping a food diary can be a powerful tool for noticing patterns and effects over time. Maybe you've noticed that yogurt with berries works great as a late-night snack now, whereas a few years ago, a piece of cheese did the job.

Understanding and adapting is the core of managing diabetes effectively through snacking. Aim to see snacks not as mere fillers but as integral, enjoyable components of your dietary regime that offer both pleasure and power—power to control your blood sugar and enjoy your lifestyle without compromise. Creating a smart snacking habit is just like gardening in many ways—it requires planning, nurturing, and continuous adjustment. Plant the right seeds with your snack choices, and you'll cultivate a daily routine that keeps you both healthy and content. With each mindful snack, you're not just quelling hunger; you're enhancing your health, bite by bite.

3. Tips for Dining Out

Navigating the dining out experience while managing diabetes after 60 can seem daunting at first glance. The ambiance, the variety, the company—it all adds up to a delightful outing, but the uncertainty around food choices might dampen your spirit. With the right approach, however, dining out can remain one of your most cherished activities, offering both the pleasure of social interaction and the enjoyment of a meal made outside your kitchen.

Let's explore how you can relish these experiences without feeling anxious about your blood sugar levels or dietary restrictions.

Start with a Plan

Imagine you're planning to visit a new restaurant with family. Before stepping out, take a peek at the menu online. Many restaurants offer their menus on their websites, allowing you to strategize your meal choices ahead of time. Look for dishes rich in vegetables, lean proteins, and whole grains. If the descriptions are vague or the menu isn't available, consider calling the restaurant. Most are more than willing to discuss their dishes or accommodate special dietary requests.

Sometimes, deciding what to eat before you arrive could save you from the all-too-common menu panic, ensuring you make a thoughtful choice that aligns with your health goals.

Communicating with The Staff

Once you arrive, don't hesitate to converse with the restaurant staff. A simple discussion with your server can result in helpful adjustments to your meal. Requesting that dressings or sauces be served on the side, opting for steamed vs. sautéed vegetables, or inquiring about portion sizes are all sensible strategies.

Consider the example of Marjorie, a retired school teacher with a fondness for dining out. Whenever she visits a restaurant, she charmingly chats with her server, explaining her preference for low-sugar options and her need to know certain ingredients due to her diabetes. Her experience has shown that when communicated respectfully, her requests are met with helpful responses and a willingness to accommodate.

The Art of Choosing Wisely

Navigating a menu requires a strategy, focusing on how various dishes are cooked and what they contain. Opt for grilled, baked, steamed, or roasted dishes, and steer clear of anything described as crispy, breaded, or fried. These cooking methods typically suggest a higher fat and calorie content, which might disrupt your blood sugar management.

If the meals seem overly generous, consider portion control at the outset: ask for a half portion, share a dish with someone else, or request a to-go container early and set aside part of your meal for later. This last strategy allows you to enjoy the palatability of your dish without overindulging.

Savor, Don't Rush

Dining out is as much about the experience as it is about the food. Engage in conversations, take in the ambiance, and truly savor each bite. Eating slowly can help you better digest your food and pay attention to your body's satiety cues, which can prevent overeating. Remember, your meal is not just about nourishing your body but also about enjoying the moment and creating memories with your dining companions.

Watching the Beverages

It's easy to forget that what we drink during a meal can also impact our blood sugar levels. Beverages like sodas, sweetened teas, or cocktails can contain high amounts of sugars and calories. Opting for water, unsweetened tea, or a glass of red wine can enhance your meal while keeping your sugar intake in check.

Handling Dessert

Dessert doesn't have to be off-limits. If you fancy something sweet to finish your meal, look for options like a fruit bowl or share a dessert with the table. This allows you to partake in the full dining experience without feeling deprived.

Reflect and Adjust

Each dining out experience is an opportunity to learn more about how different foods and the dining environment affect your blood sugar levels. After your meal, take some time to reflect on how you feel and check your blood sugar levels. This can help you understand which choices worked well and what adjustments you might need to consider for future outings. By transforming dining out into a deliberate and enjoyable component of your diabetes management strategy, you ensure that each meal out serves not just your social and emotional needs but aligns with your health goals. The key is preparation, communication, and moderation, allowing you to appreciate the best of both worlds—the joy of a great meal and the comfort in knowing you're taking care of your health in a bustling, beautiful world.

4. MONITORING AND ADAPTING TO BLOOD SUGAR CHANGES

Stepping into the world of diabetes management especially after 60, often involves equipping oneself not just with the right foods, but with the right knowledge and tools to monitor and adapt to the fluctuations of blood sugar. Understanding your body's response to different foods, activities, and stressors is crucial. Hence, establishing a routine for monitoring blood sugar and adapting your lifestyle accordingly isn't just beneficial; it's essential.

The Continuous Dialogue with Your Body

Think of monitoring your blood sugar as having an ongoing conversation with your body, where it tells you how it reacts to different inputs—food, exercise, stress, and medication. This dialogue is foundational, determining how well you manage diabetes and maintain a lifestyle that supports your overall health.

Engage in this process by regularly checking your blood sugar levels at various times – upon waking, before and after meals, before bedtime. This might sound daunting, but with modern technology, it's become increasingly hassle-free. Devices like continuous glucose monitors (CGMs) can provide real-time feedback without the need for constant finger-pricking, offering a comprehensive picture of how your glucose levels change throughout the day.

Crafting Your Response Through Data

Armed with data, you can begin to notice patterns and understand the nuances of your body's responses. It's somewhat like being a detective in a mystery novel, where every new piece of evidence can lead to better management strategies. For instance, you might discover that your blood sugar spikes every Tuesday night. A bit of reflection could reveal that it's pizza night with the grandchildren causing the spike. With this insight, you could decide to modify the amount of pizza you consume, or perhaps adjust what you eat during the day to accommodate this weekly treat.

These insights don't demand drastic changes. Often, it's the small, strategic tweaks that make the most significant difference. It could be as simple as walking around the block after meals or adjusting the timing of your medications. The key is to use the information gathered to make informed decisions that help level your blood sugar.

Adapting With Age and Experience

As we age, the body's needs and responses can change, and what worked once might not be as effective. Regular consultations with your healthcare provider can help refine your diabetes management plan as you age. During these visits, discuss any new patterns or concerns you've noticed in your blood sugar readings. Perhaps you've been more active in the community garden and need to adjust your carbohydrate intake on those days. These appointments are your opportunity to recalibrate and refine your approach based on the accumulated data and your current lifestyle.

Embracing Technological Aids

In an age where technology advances daily, several tools can aid you in managing day-to-day glucose levels. Smartphone apps can log your food intake and exercise, merging this data with your glucose levels to provide actionable insights. Also, many modern glucometers connect directly to your phone, storing and analyzing data over time to help you and your healthcare provider notice trends and make adjustments as necessary.

Lifestyle Synergy: Merging Diet, Exercise, and Monitoring

Integrating your monitoring with other aspects of your lifestyle changes, such as diet and exercise, forms a holistic approach to diabetes management. For example, if you know that brisk walking lowers your blood sugar effectively, you can plan your walks for after your meals, turning them into a tool for immediate blood sugar control.

Moreover, use what you learn from your blood sugar patterns to engage more meaningfully with your meal planning. If certain foods cause significant spikes, you might decide to replace them with others that are more blood-sugar-friendly. This doesn't mean giving up all your favorites but rather finding a balance that respects both your health and your palate.

The Emotional and Psychological Component

Monitoring your blood sugar might bring up feelings of frustration or discouragement at times. Remember, each reading is a piece of information, not a judgement. Cultivating a mindset where you view this process as informative rather than punitive can help reduce stress, which, in itself, can benefit your glucose control. Each high or low is a learning opportunity, a chance to understand your body better and give it what it needs. Just like an old friend, getting to know your body's ways can sometimes be complex, but it's always rewarding. In essence, monitoring and adapting to your blood sugar fluctuations is a dynamic and integral part of managing diabetes in your golden years. It empowers you to make informed decisions that refine your diet, modify your physical activity, and optimize your overall approach to diabetes management, ensuring that you continue to enjoy a rich, vibrant life. With every check, every number logged, and every pattern deciphered, you're not just managing diabetes; you're mastering it, one glucose reading at a time.

MACRONUTRIENTS AND MICRONUTRIENTS

1. THE ROLE OF CARBOHYDRATES AND FIBER

As we gracefully advance into our sixties and beyond, every bite and every choice in our diet becomes increasingly impactful, particularly when managing conditions like diabetes. Many of us grew up at a time when carbohydrates were either seen as the body's primary source of energy or as a villain in the world of dieting. Yet, the truth lies somewhere in the middle, especially for those of us looking to manage diabetes effectively while maintaining a zest for life's delicious pleasures.

Carbohydrates are often discussed in a rather simplistic black-and-white manner. However, the role they play in a diabetic diet is nuanced and vital for our overall health. It's not just about reducing quantities; it's about choosing the right types of carbohydrates that can help us manage blood sugar levels more effectively. These types, predominantly found in whole, unprocessed foods, include complex carbohydrates equipped with ample fiber.

Think about fiber as your ally in the journey through managing diabetes after 60. Unlike other carbohydrate types that break down into glucose, fiber doesn't cause your blood sugar to spike. It passes through the body undigested, helping to regulate the body's use of sugars, keeping hunger and blood sugar in check. This becomes fundamental in crafting a diet that doesn't just aim to manage diabetes but also enhances your overall quality of life.

Let's walk through a typical morning to see how choosing the right carbohydrates and incorporating fiber can make a significant difference. Imagine starting your day with a bowl of refined cereal; sure, it's quick and convenient, but it's also likely to cause a rapid increase and then a steep fall in blood sugar levels. Now, picture instead beginning with a warm bowl of oatmeal topped with fresh berries and a sprinkle of ground flaxseed. This meal, rich in fiber, will release glucose into your bloodstream gradually, providing a steady energy level that lasts throughout the morning.

This effective management through fiber-rich foods comes not just from the selection of what to eat, but understanding the impact of that selection. Foods high in soluble fiber, such as barley, nuts, seeds, beans, lentils, and some fruits and vegetables, can lower blood glucose levels by improving insulin sensitivity. Adding these to your diet isn't overly complex. It often involves small, manageable adjustments like choosing brown rice over white rice or opting for whole-grain bread instead of a baguette.

Such choices not only stabilize blood sugar but also contribute to a feeling of fullness after meals. This sensation of satiety can curb the common craving swings that many experience, which, in turn, helps manage weight—a crucial element in diabetes management. Another factor often overlooked in the conversation about carbohydrates and fibers in a diabetic diet is their collective impact on gut health. A diet rich in high-fiber foods can promote a healthier gut microbiome, which plays a critical role in everything from digestion to immune function. Emerging research suggests that a healthy gut can also affect how your body responds to insulin, further influencing diabetes management.

Now, as we gather together at family meals or dine out with friends, the challenge often lies in making choices that align with these principles without feeling isolated by your dietary needs. It's about finding a balance where your meal remains a pleasure without becoming a source of stress due to its sugar content. Opting for fiber-rich foods becomes not just a medical advice but a choice towards longer, more satisfying conversations around the dinner table, without the nagging worry of a blood sugar spike.

To integrate these principles into your everyday life, start by gradually increasing your fiber intake, giving your body time to adjust. Include a variety of sources to not only prevent boredom but to cover a broader spectrum of nutrients. Discuss your carbohydrate choices with your healthcare provider or a dietitian to tailor your diet closer to your personal medical needs and preferences.

In managing diabetes post-60, equipping yourself with the knowledge of what carbohydrates work in your favor and how fiber plays into this can transform your approach from one of limitation to one of empowerment. Embrace these choices with enthusiasm, knowing each step you take is building towards a healthier, vibrant life where you can enjoy the pleasures of good food with less worry about your health.

In sum, understanding and choosing the right types of carbohydrates and ensuring adequate fiber intake are not just dietary choices—they are integral to managing diabetes effectively, preventing complications, and enjoying a thriving, joyful life even after 60.

2. CHOOSING HEALTHY FATS

Navigating the maze of dietary advice can sometimes feel overwhelming, especially when it comes to fats. For decades, fats were virtually vilified. Yet in our golden years, particularly as we manage conditions like diabetes, understanding and choosing the right types of fats can make a substantial difference, not only for our blood sugar levels but for overall vitality and well-being.

Let's meander through the concept of fats with the ease of old friends chatting over a cup of tea. You might recall the days when margarine was all the rage, believed to be a healthier alternative to butter. Fast forward to our contemporary knowledge, and we now comprehend the complexity of fats much better. It turns out, not all fats are foes. Some, in fact, are essential allies, aiding in nutrient absorption, nerve transmission, and the maintenance of cell membranes.

Healthy fats, particularly unsaturated fats, are a cornerstone of a balanced diet for managing diabetes effectively. These are the fats found in avocados, nuts, seeds, and olive oil. Picture yourself drizzling a bit of extra virgin olive oil over a crisp, colorful salad. Not only does it enhance the flavor, but it also helps your body manage inflammation and maintains the health of your heart. This is especially crucial since diabetes can heighten cardiovascular risk.

Then, there is the often-discussed omega-3 fatty acids. Predominantly found in fish like salmon and mackerel, these fats are champions at protecting heart health. For someone managing diabetes, omega-3s can be particularly beneficial, helping reduce episodes of erratic heart rhythms and lowering blood pressure levels, liabilities that tend to accompany diabetes.

Remember how we used to enjoy those catch-of-the-day dinners by the seaside? Incorporating similar meals into our weekly routine isn't just about reliving those memories; it's about taking proactive steps to enrich our diet with fats that support our health.

Of course, moderation is key in everything, particularly when it involves dietary fats. While fats are essential, they are also dense in calories, which means mindful consumption is necessary to maintain a healthy weight. Think about using avocado as a spread on your whole-grain toast—delicious and far healthier than many store-bought spreads infused with trans fats and excessive sodium.

Trans fats, on the other hand, are the real culprits to watch out for. These are typically found in processed foods and baked goods. They're cheap and extend the shelf life of products, but they wreak havoc on our body, particularly aggravating insulin resistance, which is something we certainly want to avoid. Steering clear of trans fats means reading labels diligently when shopping. If the ingredient list includes "partially hydrogenated oils," it's probably best to put it back on the shelf. Let's also chat about saturated fats. These are the types primarily found in animal products like meat and dairy. While not as harmful as trans fats, consuming them in high amounts can lead to health issues like elevated cholesterol levels. An approach I find sensible is to enjoy these foods in moderation. Savor that steak during a family barbecue, but balance it with plenty of fiber-rich vegetables and healthy fats like olive oil-based dressings.

Transitioning to healthier fats doesn't have to be a bland or distressing endeavor. In fact, it can be quite pleasurable. Imagine replacing the cream in your coffee with a splash of almond or oat milk. Not only does this simple swap allow you to enjoy your morning brew guilt-free, but it also introduces a delightful new taste experience.

The relationship between fats and diabetes management is not centered around exclusion but rather about making informed choices that enhance flavor and fortify our health. Integrating healthy fats into our diet helps smooth out blood sugar fluctuations and bolsters our energy—two critical factors in managing diabetes.

Simply put, as you stand before your pantry or refrigerator, think of fats as tools in your culinary toolkit. Opt for oils that are friends of your heart and waistline, nuts that can replace less healthy snacks without forgoing the pleasure of a crispy bite, and fish that brings the sea's bounty to your plate, nourishing your body while delighting your palate.

Through conscientious choices, the journey to manage diabetes after 60 with smart fat consumption becomes not just achievable but also enjoyable. This way, we ensure that our later years are not spent in deprivation, but in savoring each meal and moment, fortified with the knowledge that we are doing the best for our health without sacrificing joy and taste. Thus, as we select our fats with care, we pave the way for a life full of flavor and vigor, proving that a diet rich in the right nutrients is a cornerstone of living well with diabetes.

3. Proteins for Muscle Maintenance

In the journey of managing diabetes after 60, it's not just what's on our plate that matters, but how the elements of that plate help us sustain our vitality and muscle strength. Among the essential nutrients, proteins stand out as fundamental pillars supporting muscle maintenance, a crucial aspect as we age.

When we talk about protein, we often imagine bodybuilders and athletes huddled over plates of chicken and shakes. But proteins are just as critical for retirees and senior citizens looking to maintain a healthy lifestyle while managing diabetes. Proteins do more than build and repair muscle; they help stabilize blood sugar levels by slowing the absorption of sugar during meals, making it an invaluable nutrient for those with diabetes.

Imagine a tapestry delicately woven with various threads, each thread representing a different aspect of our health supported by protein. This could include hormone production, immune response, and the ongoing repair of tissue, along with maintaining muscle mass, which naturally depreciates as we grow older. This loss of muscle mass, known medically as sarcopenia, can significantly impact our mobility and independence—factors integral to a quality life in our later years.

Now, visualize your life as a leisurely stroll through a garden. Each step represents a day in the journey of managing diabetes. Every morning, you have the opportunity to stabilize your stroll—your blood sugar—by selecting the right type of protein. Whether it's a handful of almonds, a slice of turkey breast, or a serving of Greek yogurt, these choices contribute not just to immediate blood sugar management but to sustaining your muscle mass and by extension, your independence.

While proteins are abundant and varied—from plant-based varieties like lentils and quinoa to animal-based options such as poultry and fish—understanding the concept of complete and incomplete proteins is vital. Complete proteins contain all nine essential amino acids necessary for bodily function, typically found in animal products. However, plant-based proteins often lack one or more of these amino acids, hence termed incomplete.

The beauty of nutrition lies in its flexibility and adaptability. For those of us leaning towards a plant-based diet, combining different protein sources throughout the day can ensure that we receive all the essential amino acids our bodies require. This could be as simple as pairing brown rice with black beans or enjoying whole grain bread with peanut butter.

Reflecting on the importance of dietary choices brings to mind the story of a dear friend. Having been diagnosed with type 2 diabetes, he faced significant challenges in managing his condition. His journey turned a corner when he shifted his focus towards a balanced diet rich in robust proteins. Integrating lean meat, fish, and a variety of legumes helped him not only stabilize his blood sugar but also reclaim strength that he thought had been lost to age. This approach aligns with the broader spectrum of maintaining a healthy weight and metabolism, which are pivotal in the overall diabetes management strategy. Proteins have a higher thermic effect, meaning they can increase metabolic rate more than fats or carbohydrates. This is important for those of us in our senior years when metabolism tends to slow down.

Incorporating adequate protein into our diet is not about redefining eating habits entirely but refining them in ways that maintain the joy and essence of eating. It could be as satisfying as enjoying a roasted chicken with herbs for dinner or as refreshing as sipping on a smoothie blended with whey protein after a morning walk. Yet, as with any nutrient, balance is crucial. Excessive protein intake, particularly animal protein, can strain kidneys, and for those among us with diabetic kidney complications, this is a significant consideration. It's about choosing the right amount and the right kind of protein—prioritizing lean sources, both animal and plant-based, that can support our health without undue stress on the body.

Ultimately, proteins are not just a part of our diet; they are a vital component of our lifestyle, a cornerstone supporting our bodies and our zest for life. Embracing protein in our diet is less about following a trend and more about crafting a tailor-made approach that honors our bodies' needs, enhances our health, and prolongs our vitality. As we gather with family, dine with friends, or enjoy a quiet meal alone, let protein be not just a guest on your plate but a companion on your journey of health and diabetes management. Each meal, then, becomes not just a part of daily routine but an investment in a vibrant, active future.

4. Essential Vitamins and Minerals for Diabetes

Embarking on the golden years, we often find ourselves paying more attention to the intricacies of our health—an endeavor that becomes particularly significant when managing diabetes. Beyond macronutrients like carbohydrates, fats, and proteins, our bodies crave a symphony of vitamins and minerals that play crucial roles not only in managing blood sugar levels but in maintaining overall vitality.

As we unwrap the tapestry of nutrients essential for our well-being, think of vitamins and minerals as the delicate yet robust threads interwoven throughout, each contributing uniquely toward our physiological melodies. Managing diabetes effectively requires a keen understanding of how these nutrients support our body's needs, potentially reducing complications and enhancing life's quality and zest.

Consider, for instance, the might of magnesium. This mineral is a stalwart ally in the diabetic diet, instrumental in regulating blood sugar levels. Found in abundantly in leafy greens, nuts, and seeds, magnesium aids the body's ability to use insulin effectively. Imagine enjoying a crisp spinach salad sprinkled with almonds—a simple yet profoundly beneficial meal for a diabetic diet, combining taste with a nutritional boost for your blood sugar control.

Next, let's dive into the world of antioxidants—vitamins C and E. These are like the body's own personal bodyguards, protecting cells from damage, which is particularly crucial when you've diabetes. Vitamin C, apart from its immune-boosting qualities, helps in repairing tissues and enzymatic production of certain neurotransmitters. Peppers, citrus fruits, and tomatoes are not just explosions of flavor on the palate; they are also rich in this powerful antioxidant. Similarly, vitamin E, with its properties to combat oxidative stress, can be easily sourced from nuts and vegetable oils, making it an easy addition to our daily diet.

Not forgetting the B-vitamins, which include folic acid, vitamin B6, and B12—a trio known for their role in maintaining optimal nerve health, which is pivotal considering diabetic neuropathy. Legumes, whole grains, and bananas are excellent sources of these vitamins, providing a delicious means to fortify nerve health and keep various diabetes-related complications at bay.

Another vital player in the diabetic health arena is zinc. This mineral helps in the synthesis of insulin, which is a cornerstone for diabetes management. Foods like seafood, beef, and legumes are not only rich in zinc but also belong to a palette of robust flavors, enhancing meals while fortifying your health.

Ironically, while the essence of managing diabetes often concentrates on insulin and sugar levels, calcium plays a quietly formidable role. Necessary for strong bones, optimal nerve transmission, and muscle function, calcium, together with vitamin D, ensures that each signal in your body from your brain to your toes is crisp and clear. Dairy products, fortified plant milk, and leafy greens provide a delectable array of choices for keeping calcium levels up.

Now, embracing these nutrients might feel akin to stepping into the sunlight after a long, dark winter. The warmth is invigorating but can be overwhelming without a guide. Here lies the importance of integrating these vitamins and minerals thoughtfully and intentionally into daily meals, considering the big picture of a diabetic diet.

However, maxing out on supplements is not the golden ticket. The ultimate goal is achieving a balanced diet where these nutrients naturally occur, ensuring their bioavailability and effectiveness. This approach not only enhances the absorption of these vitamins and minerals but also adds an array of colors, textures, and flavors to the plate, making each meal a celebration rather than a mere nutritional requirement.

Reflecting on all these nutrients, consider the vibrant variety of foods as your toolkit. Each meal is an opportunity to paint your health canvas with broad strokes of vibrant veggies, wholesome grains, lean proteins, and heart-healthy fats, dotted with the meticulous detailing of essential vitamins and minerals.

In the narratives of our lives, meals are poignant moments of connection—both within our bodies and with each other. They are opportunities to nourish not just our cells but our souls. Managing diabetes in our later years with a diet rich in essential vitamins and minerals transforms the challenge into a lifestyle of mindfulness and richness. This isn't merely about adding days to our life, but life to our days, ensuring every moment is lived with health, happiness, and flavor.

BREAKFAST

1. Low-Carb Morning Staples

Spinach and Feta Breakfast Scramble

PREPARATION TIME: 10 min

COOKING TIME: 15 min

MODE OF COOKING: Sautéing

INGREDIENTS:

- 4 large eggs
- 2 cups fresh spinach leaves
- 1/2 cup crumbled feta cheese
- 1 Tbsp olive oil
- 1/4 cup diced onions
- Salt and pepper to taste

DIRECTIONS:

1. Heat olive oil in a non-stick skillet over medium heat.
2. Sauté onions until translucent, about 3-4 minutes.
3. Add spinach to the skillet and cook until just wilted, about 2-3 minutes.
4. Beat the eggs in a bowl and pour them over the spinach and onions.
5. Cook without stirring for about 1 minute, then gently stir to scramble.
6. When eggs are nearly set, sprinkle feta cheese over the scramble.
7. Cook for another 1-2 minutes, allowing the feta to slightly melt and the eggs to fully set.

8. Season with salt and pepper to taste and serve immediately.

TIPS:
- For added flavor, sprinkle a pinch of dried oregano or basil in the eggs before cooking.
- Serve with a slice of whole-grain toast for a more filling meal.

NUTRITIONAL VALUES: Calories: 220, Fat: 16g, Carbs: 4g, Protein: 14g, Sugar: 2g, Glycemic Index (GI): Low

SMOKED SALMON AND AVOCADO SALAD

PREPARATION TIME: 10 min
COOKING TIME: 0 min
MODE OF COOKING: No cook
INGREDIENTS:
- 4 oz smoked salmon, sliced
- 1 ripe avocado, cubed
- 2 cups mixed greens (arugula, spinach, kale)
- 1/2 cucumber, sliced
- 1 Tbsp extra-virgin olive oil
- 1 lemon, juiced
- Salt and pepper to taste

DIRECTIONS:
1. In a large salad bowl, combine mixed greens, cucumber slices, and avocado cubes.
2. Top with slices of smoked salmon.
3. Drizzle with olive oil and fresh lemon juice.
4. Toss gently to mix the ingredients.
5. Season with salt and pepper to taste and serve immediately.

TIPS:
- You can add some toasted almond slivers for a crunchy texture.
- A sprinkle of dill enhances the flavors, especially with salmon.

NUTRITIONAL VALUES: Calories: 240, Fat: 18g, Carbs: 8g, Protein: 12g, Sugar: 2g, Glycemic Index (GI): Low

CAULIFLOWER HASH BROWNS

PREPARATION TIME: 15 min
COOKING TIME: 15 min
MODE OF COOKING: Pan-frying
INGREDIENTS:

- 2 cups riced cauliflower
- 1/4 cup shredded cheddar cheese
- 1 large egg
- 2 Tbsp almond flour
- 1 Tbsp olive oil
- Salt and pepper to taste

DIRECTIONS:

1. In a mixing bowl, combine riced cauliflower, cheddar cheese, egg, and almond flour.
2. Season with salt and pepper and mix until well combined.
3. Heat olive oil in a skillet over medium heat.
4. Scoop portions of the cauliflower mixture and form into small patties.
5. Fry each patty for 3-4 minutes per side or until golden brown and crispy.
6. Remove from skillet and drain on paper towels.

TIPS:

- Ensure the cauliflower is dry by squeezing out excess moisture with a clean kitchen towel.
- Serve with a dollop of low-fat Greek yogurt or sugar-free ketchup.

NUTRITIONAL VALUES: Calories: 130, Fat: 9g, Carbs: 5g, Protein: 6g, Sugar: 2g, Glycemic Index (GI): Low

GREEK YOGURT AND BERRY PARFAIT

PREPARATION TIME: 5 min

COOKING TIME: 0 min

MODE OF COOKING: No cook

INGREDIENTS:

- 1 cup plain Greek yogurt
- 1/2 cup mixed berries (blueberries, strawberries, raspberries)
- 1 Tbsp flaxseeds
- 1 tsp stevia (optional)

DIRECTIONS:

1. In a serving glass, layer half of the Greek yogurt.
2. Add a layer of mixed berries and sprinkle with half of the flaxseeds.
3. Add the remaining yogurt followed by the remaining berries and flaxseeds.
4. Sprinkle with stevia for added sweetness, if desired.

TIPS:

- For a crunchier texture, add a few almond slivers or chia seeds between layers.
- Ensure all ingredients are chilled for a refreshing morning start.

NUTRITIONAL VALUES: Calories: 180, Fat: 4g, Carbs: 15g, Protein: 20g, Sugar: 9g, Glycemic Index (GI): Low

TOFU AND VEGETABLE STIR-FRY

PREPARATION TIME: 10 min

COOKING TIME: 10 min

MODE OF COOKING: Stir-frying

INGREDIENTS:

- 1/2 lb firm tofu, cubed
- 1 cup broccoli florets
- 1/2 bell pepper, sliced
- 1 carrot, thinly sliced
- 2 Tbsp soy sauce (low sodium)
- 1 Tbsp olive oil
- 1 tsp ginger, minced

DIRECTIONS:
1. Heat olive oil in a large skillet or wok over medium-high heat.
2. Add ginger and sauté for 1 minute.
3. Add broccoli, bell pepper, and carrots, stir-frying for about 5 minutes until vegetables are just tender.
4. Add tofu cubes and soy sauce; continue to stir-fry for another 5 minutes until tofu is heated through and slightly browned.
5. Serve hot.

TIPS:
- Press tofu for at least 30 minutes before cooking to remove excess moisture and improve texture.
- A splash of sesame oil before serving can add a rich, nutty flavor.

NUTRITIONAL VALUES: Calories: 200, Fat: 12g, Carbs: 10g, Protein: 16g, Sugar: 3g, Glycemic Index (GI): Low

2. SWEET YET SUGAR-FREE MORNINGS

Cinnamon Apple Chia Pudding

PREPARATION TIME: 15 min

COOKING TIME: 0 min (requires overnight refrigeration)

MODE OF COOKING: Refrigeration

INGREDIENTS:

- 1/4 cup chia seeds
- 1 cup unsweetened almond milk
- 1 tsp cinnamon
- 1/2 tsp pure vanilla extract
- 1 large green apple, grated
- 1 Tbsp almond butter, no added sugar
- Optional: a pinch of stevia for added sweetness

DIRECTIONS:

1. In a mixing bowl, combine the chia seeds and almond milk, stirring until the chia seeds are evenly dispersed and beginning to swell.
2. Add cinnamon, vanilla extract, and stevia if using, mixing thoroughly to incorporate.
3. Cover the bowl and refrigerate overnight, allowing the chia seeds to fully hydrate and form a pudding-like consistency.
4. The next morning, stir the pudding well. If it's too thick, add a little more almond milk to reach your desired consistency.
5. Fold the grated green apple and almond butter into the pudding.
6. Serve chilled, with an optional sprinkle of cinnamon on top.

TIPS:

- Top with a few walnuts or sliced almonds for a crunchy texture.
- If you prefer a smoother pudding, blend the mixture before adding the grated apple.
- For a warmer breakfast option, gently heat the pudding on the stove before adding the apple and almond butter.

NUTRITIONAL VALUES: Calories: 275, Fat: 17g, Carbs: 24g, Protein: 6g, Sugar: 10g, Glycemic Index (GI): Low

BERRY YOGHURT SMOOTHIE BOWL

PREPARATION TIME: 10 min
COOKING TIME: 0 min
MODE OF COOKING: Blending
INGREDIENTS:

- 1/2 cup unsweetened Greek yogurt
- 1/2 cup frozen mixed berries (blueberries, raspberries, strawberries)
- 1/4 avocado, peeled and pitted
- 1 Tbsp flaxseeds
- 1/4 cup unsweetened almond milk
- Optional: a pinch of stevia for added sweetness

DIRECTIONS:

1. Place the Greek yogurt, frozen berries, avocado, and flaxseeds in a blender.
2. Add the almond milk; you can adjust the quantity to achieve your desired texture.
3. Blend on high until the mixture is smooth and creamy.
4. Pour the smoothie mixture into a bowl.
5. Garnish with a few whole berries, a sprinkle of chia seeds, and a drizzle of almond butter.

TIPS:

- Ensure your berries are frozen to give the bowl a thick, ice-cream-like consistency.
- Add a scoop of protein powder for an added protein boost.

NUTRITIONAL VALUES: Calories: 300, Fat: 15g, Carbs: 26g, Protein: 12g, Sugar: 12g, Glycemic Index (GI): Low

Fluffy Cottage Cheese Pancakes

PREPARATION TIME: 10 min

COOKING TIME: 10 min

MODE OF COOKING: Pan-frying

INGREDIENTS:

- 1/2 cup low-fat cottage cheese
- 2 eggs
- 1/4 cup almond flour
- 1/2 tsp baking powder
- 1/2 tsp vanilla extract
- Cooking spray or a dab of butter for the pan

DIRECTIONS:

1. In a blender, combine the cottage cheese, eggs, almond flour, baking powder, and vanilla extract.
2. Blend until the mixture is smooth.
3. Heat a non-stick frying pan over medium heat and lightly grease with cooking spray or butter.
4. Pour small rounds of batter onto the hot pan. Cook for about 2-3 minutes on each side or until golden brown and fluffy.
5. Serve hot with a dollop of Greek yogurt and a sprinkle of cinnamon.

TIPS:

- Add a handful of fresh berries to the batter for a fruity variation.
- These pancakes can be made in advance and reheated for a quick breakfast.

NUTRITIONAL VALUES: Calories: 280, Fat: 15g, Carbs: 12g, Protein: 22g, Sugar: 4g, Glycemic Index (GI): Medium-Low

SPINACH AND MUSHROOM OMELETTE

PREPARATION TIME: 5 min
COOKING TIME: 10 min
MODE OF COOKING: Sautéing and frying
INGREDIENTS:
- 2 large eggs
- 1 cup fresh spinach, chopped
- 1/2 cup mushrooms, sliced
- 1 Tbsp olive oil
- 2 Tbsp feta cheese, crumbled
- Salt and pepper to taste

DIRECTIONS:
1. Heat the olive oil in a skillet over medium heat.
2. Add the mushrooms and sauté until they are soft and browned, about 4-5 minutes.
3. Add the spinach and cook until it wilts, about 1-2 minutes.
4. In a bowl, whisk the eggs with salt and pepper.
5. Pour the eggs over the sautéed vegetables in the skillet, tilting the pan to ensure an even spread.
6. Sprinkle the feta cheese over the top.
7. Cook until the edges start to lift from the pan, then fold the omelette in half.
8. Serve hot.

TIPS:
- Add a pinch of nutmeg to the egg mixture for enhanced flavor.
- Serve with a side of sliced avocado for extra healthy fats.

NUTRITIONAL VALUES: Calories: 320, Fat: 25g, Carbs: 5g, Protein: 19g, Sugar: 2g, Glycemic Index (GI): Low

GRAPEFRUIT AND AVOCADO SALAD

PREPARATION TIME: 10 min

COOKING TIME: 0 min

MODE OF COOKING: Assembling

INGREDIENTS:

- 1 large grapefruit, peeled and sectioned
- 1 avocado, peeled and sliced
- 2 cups mixed greens (spinach, arugula, kale)
- 1 Tbsp extra-virgin olive oil
- 1 tsp apple cider vinegar
- Salt and pepper to taste

DIRECTIONS:

1. In a large bowl, place the mixed greens.
2. Top the greens with grapefruit sections and avocado slices.
3. In a small bowl, whisk together the olive oil, apple cider vinegar, salt, and pepper.
4. Drizzle the dressing over the salad and gently toss to coat.

TIPS:

- Add a sprinkle of chia seeds or flaxseeds for a nutty flavor and extra nutrients.
- This salad pairs beautifully with grilled salmon or chicken for a heartier meal.

NUTRITIONAL VALUES: Calories: 250, Fat: 20g, Carbs: 18g, Protein: 3g, Sugar: 12g, Glycemic Index (GI): Low

LUNCH

1. POWER SALADS AND BOWLS

Mediterranean Tuna and Bean Salad

PREPARATION TIME: 15 min

COOKING TIME: 0 min

MODE OF COOKING: No cook

INGREDIENTS:

- 2 cans (6 oz each) of tuna in water, drained
- 1 can (15 oz) of cannellini beans, rinsed and drained
- 1 large cucumber, diced
- 1 red bell pepper, diced
- 1/4 cup red onion, finely chopped
- 1/4 cup flat-leaf parsley, chopped
- 2 Tbsp extra-virgin olive oil
- 2 Tbsp lemon juice
- 1 tsp dried oregano
- Salt and pepper to taste

DIRECTIONS:

1. In a large bowl, combine the drained tuna, cannellini beans, cucumber, red bell pepper, red onion, and parsley.
2. In a small bowl, whisk together the olive oil, lemon juice, oregano, salt, and pepper.

3. Pour the dressing over the tuna and bean mixture and toss gently to combine.
4. Let the salad chill in the refrigerator for at least 10 minutes before serving to allow flavors to meld.

TIPS:
- For added zest, include a tablespoon of capers.
- Serve chilled on a bed of mixed greens for a complete meal.
- Perfect for meal prep, keeps well in the refrigerator for up to 3 days.

NUTRITIONAL VALUES: Calories: 230, Fat: 8g, Carbs: 20g, Protein: 22g, Sugar: 3g, Glycemic Index (GI): Low

SPICY SHRIMP AND AVOCADO SALAD

PREPARATION TIME: 20 min
COOKING TIME: 5 min
MODE OF COOKING: Sautéing
INGREDIENTS:
- 1 lb shrimp, peeled and deveined
- 1 Tbsp olive oil
- 1 tsp smoked paprika
- 1/2 tsp garlic powder
- 2 avocados, cubed
- 1 cup cherry tomatoes, halved
- 1/4 cup red onion, thinly sliced
- 1 jalapeño, seeded and finely chopped
- Juice of 1 lime
- Salt and pepper to taste
- Fresh cilantro for garnish

DIRECTIONS:
1. Heat the olive oil in a large skillet over medium heat.
2. Season the shrimp with smoked paprika, garlic powder, salt, and pepper.
3. Sauté the shrimp for 2-3 minutes on each side until pink and cooked through.
4. In a large salad bowl, combine the cooked shrimp, avocado, cherry tomatoes, red onion, and jalapeño.

5. Squeeze lime juice over the salad and toss gently to combine.
6. Garnish with fresh cilantro before serving.

TIPS:
- Adjust the amount of jalapeño according to your spice preference.
- This salad can be served over a bed of quinoa for a hearty meal.
- For best flavor, use freshly squeezed lime juice.

NUTRITIONAL VALUES: Calories: 295, Fat: 15g, Carbs: 12g, Protein: 27g, Sugar: 2g, Glycemic Index (GI): Low

2. HEARTY YET HEALTHY MAINS

Zesty Lemon Herb Grilled Salmon

PREPARATION TIME: 20 min

COOKING TIME: 15 min

MODE OF COOKING: Grilling

INGREDIENTS:

- 4 salmon fillets (6 oz. each)
- 2 Tbsp olive oil
- 1 lemon, juiced and zested
- 2 cloves garlic, minced
- 1 Tbsp fresh dill, chopped
- 1 Tbsp fresh parsley, chopped
- Salt and pepper to taste

PROCEDURE:

1. In a small bowl, whisk together the olive oil, lemon juice, lemon zest, minced garlic, dill, parsley, salt, and pepper.
2. Place the salmon fillets in a shallow dish and pour the marinade over them, making sure each fillet is well coated.
3. Marinate in the refrigerator for at least 10 minutes.
4. Preheat grill to medium-high heat (around 375°F or 190°C).
5. Place salmon on the grill, skin side down, and cook for 7-8 minutes per side or until the fish flakes easily with a fork.
6. Transfer to a serving dish and garnish with additional lemon slices and herbs if desired.

TIPS:

- Ensure the grill is well-oiled to prevent the fish from sticking.
- Do not overcook the salmon to maintain its moistness and flavor.

NUTRITIONAL VALUES: Calories: 280, Fat: 18g, Carbs: 1g, Protein: 28g, Sugar: 0g, Glycemic Index (GI): Low

DINNER

1. COMFORT FOODS, DIABETIC STYLE

DIABETIC-FRIENDLY STUFFED BELL PEPPERS

PREPARATION TIME: 20 min

COOKING TIME: 40 min

MODE OF COOKING: Baking

INGREDIENTS:

- 4 large bell peppers, tops cut off and seeds removed
- 1 Tbsp extra-virgin olive oil
- 1/2 lb ground turkey
- 1 cup cooked quinoa
- 1 medium onion, chopped
- 2 cloves garlic, minced
- 1 cup chopped spinach
- 1/2 cup low-fat ricotta cheese
- 1 tsp dried oregano
- Salt and pepper to taste
- 1/2 cup low-sodium vegetable broth

DIRECTIONS:

1. Preheat oven to 375°F (190°C).
2. In a skillet over medium heat, warm the olive oil and sauté onion and garlic until translucent.

3. Add ground turkey and cook until browned.
4. Stir in cooked quinoa, spinach, ricotta, oregano, salt, and pepper. Cook for an additional 3-4 minutes.
5. Stuff the bell peppers with the turkey and quinoa mixture, place them in a baking dish, and pour vegetable broth around the peppers.
6. Cover with foil and bake in the preheated oven for 35 minutes. Remove the foil and bake for another 5 minutes or until the peppers are tender.

TIPS:
- Choose different colored bell peppers for a visually appealing dish.
- For a spicier version, add a pinch of red pepper flakes to the turkey mixture.

NUTRITIONAL VALUES: Calories: 250, Fat: 10g, Carbs: 22g, Protein: 20g, Sugar: 8g, Glycemic Index (GI): Low

Lemon Herb Baked Salmon

PREPARATION TIME: 10 min
COOKING TIME: 20 min
MODE OF COOKING: Baking
INGREDIENTS:
- 4 salmon fillets (4 oz each)
- 2 Tbsp extra-virgin olive oil
- 1 lemon, juiced and zest grated
- 2 Tbsp chopped fresh parsley
- 1 Tbsp chopped fresh dill
- 1 clove garlic, minced
- Salt and pepper to taste

DIRECTIONS:
1. Preheat oven to 400°F (204°C).
2. In a small bowl, combine olive oil, lemon juice and zest, parsley, dill, garlic, salt, and pepper.
3. Place salmon fillets in a baking dish, and pour the lemon herb mixture over the salmon.
4. Bake in the preheated oven for 18-20 minutes or until salmon flakes easily with

a fork.

TIPS:
- Serve with a side of steamed green beans or asparagus for a complete meal.
- Leftovers can be flaked and added to salads or wraps for a nutritious lunch.

NUTRITIONAL VALUES: Calories: 280, Fat: 18g, Carbs: 2g, Protein: 25g, Sugar: 1g, Glycemic Index (GI): Low

CREAMY TOMATO AND SPINACH PASTA

PREPARATION TIME: 15 min
COOKING TIME: 15 min
MODE OF COOKING: Boiling/Sautéing
INGREDIENTS:
- 8 oz whole wheat pasta
- 1 Tbsp extra-virgin olive oil
- 1 onion, chopped
- 2 cloves garlic, minced
- 1 can (14 oz) sugar-free diced tomatoes
- 3 cups fresh spinach
- 1/2 cup low-fat cottage cheese
- 1 tsp dried basil
- Salt and pepper to taste

DIRECTIONS:
1. Cook pasta according to package instructions; drain and set aside.
2. In a large skillet, heat olive oil over medium heat and sauté onion and garlic until soft.
3. Add diced tomatoes with juices and bring to a simmer.
4. Stir in spinach and cook until wilted.
5. Reduce heat and blend in cottage cheese, cooked pasta, basil, salt, and pepper. Cook for an additional 2-3 minutes, stirring until well combined and heated through.

TIPS:
- Top with grated Parmesan cheese if desired.

- Substitute spinach with kale for an additional nutrient boost.

NUTRITIONAL VALUES: Calories: 280, Fat: 5g, Carbs: 46g, Protein: 14g, Sugar: 7g, Glycemic Index (GI): Medium

2. LIGHT YET SATISFYING EVENING MEALS

ZESTY LIME AND HERB GRILLED SALMON

PREPARATION TIME: 10 min

COOKING TIME: 15 min

MODE OF COOKING: Grilling

INGREDIENTS:

- 4 salmon fillets (about 6 oz. each)
- 2 Tbsp olive oil
- 1 lime, juiced and zested
- 2 garlic cloves, minced
- 1 Tbsp fresh chopped dill
- 1 Tbsp fresh chopped parsley
- Salt and pepper to taste

DIRECTIONS:

1. In a small bowl, combine olive oil, lime juice and zest, garlic, dill, parsley, salt, and pepper.
2. Place salmon fillets in a shallow dish and pour the marinade over them. Cover and marinate in the refrigerator for at least 30 min.
3. Preheat grill to medium-high heat (about 375°F or 190°C).
4. Remove salmon from marinade and grill each side for about 6-7 min or until the fish flakes easily with a fork.

TIPS:

- Ensure the grill is well-oiled to prevent the salmon from sticking.

- Serve with a side of grilled asparagus for a complete meal.

NUTRITIONAL VALUES: Calories: 280, Fat: 18g, Carbs: 2g, Protein: 26g, Sugar: 1g, Glycemic Index (GI): Low

MEDITERRANEAN STUFFED BELL PEPPERS

PREPARATION TIME: 20 min

COOKING TIME: 30 min

MODE OF COOKING: Baking

INGREDIENTS:

- 4 large bell peppers, any color
- 1 cup cooked quinoa
- 1 can (15 oz.) chickpeas, drained and rinsed
- 1 cup cherry tomatoes, halved
- 1/2 cup crumbled feta cheese
- 1/4 cup chopped kalamata olives
- 2 Tbsp olive oil
- 1 tsp dried oregano
- Salt and pepper to taste
- 1/4 cup fresh basil, chopped

DIRECTIONS:

1. Preheat oven to 375°F (190°C).
2. Cut the tops off the bell peppers and remove seeds and membranes.
3. In a bowl, combine quinoa, chickpeas, cherry tomatoes, feta cheese, olives, olive oil, oregano, salt, and pepper.
4. Stuff each bell pepper with the quinoa mixture and place in a baking dish.
5. Cover with foil and bake for about 30 min, then uncover and bake for another 10 min until the peppers are tender.
6. Garnish with fresh basil before serving.

TIPS:

- To enhance the Mediterranean flavors, add a sprinkle of lemon zest to the stuffing mixture.
- Can be served with a side salad for added freshness.

NUTRITIONAL VALUES: Calories: 290, Fat: 12g, Carbs: 38g, Protein: 12g, Sugar: 8g, Glycemic Index (GI): Medium

GINGER SOY TOFU STIR-FRY

PREPARATION TIME: 15 min
COOKING TIME: 10 min
MODE OF COOKING: Stir-frying
INGREDIENTS:

- 1 lb. firm tofu, cubed
- 2 Tbsp sesame oil
- 2 cups mixed vegetables (broccoli, carrots, bell peppers)
- 2 Tbsp soy sauce (low sodium)
- 1 Tbsp fresh grated ginger
- 2 garlic cloves, minced
- 2 tsp honey or stevia
- 1 Tbsp sesame seeds

DIRECTIONS:

1. Heat sesame oil in a large skillet or wok over medium-high heat.
2. Add tofu and cook until golden brown on all sides.
3. Add mixed vegetables, and stir-fry for about 5 min.
4. In a small bowl, mix soy sauce, ginger, garlic, and honey or stevia, then pour over the tofu and vegetables.
5. Cook for an additional 5 min, stirring frequently.
6. Sprinkle with sesame seeds before serving.

TIPS:

- For a bit of a kick, add a splash of chili sauce to the soy mixture.
- Serve over a small portion of brown rice or quinoa.

NUTRITIONAL VALUES: Calories: 210, Fat: 14g, Carbs: 12g, Protein: 12g, Sugar: 4g, Glycemic Index (GI): Low

FREE SUGAR DESSERT

1. NATURALLY SWEETENED TREATS

ALMOND & BERRY BREAKFAST TART

PREPARATION TIME: 20 min
COOKING TIME: 25 min
MODE OF COOKING: Baking
INGREDIENTS:

- 1 cup almond flour
- 1/4 cup coconut flour
- 1/3 cup melted coconut oil
- 2 Tbsp erythritol
- 1 tsp pure vanilla extract
- 1/2 tsp cinnamon
- 1 cup mixed berries (blueberries, raspberries, strawberries)
- 1/4 cup unsweetened Greek yogurt

DIRECTIONS:

1. Preheat oven to 350°F (175°C).
2. In a bowl, mix together almond flour, coconut flour, erythritol, cinnamon, and vanilla extract.
3. Add melted coconut oil to the flour mixture and stir until a dough forms.
4. Press the dough into a 9-inch tart pan and bake for 15 minutes or until slightly golden.

5. Remove from oven and let cool.
6. Once cooled, spread Greek yogurt over the crust.
7. Top with fresh mixed berries.

TIPS:
- Opt for organic or naturally grown berries to minimize pesticide exposure.
- Ensure the tart is completely cool before adding Greek yogurt to prevent it from melting.

NUTRITIONAL VALUES: Calories: 200, Fat: 15g, Carbs: 10g, Protein: 5g, Sugar: 3g, Glycemic Index (GI): Low

Cinnamon Spice Poached Pears

PREPARATION TIME: 10 min
COOKING TIME: 20 min
MODE OF COOKING: Poaching
INGREDIENTS:
- 4 green pears, peeled and cored
- 4 cups of water
- 1 cinnamon stick
- 2 cloves
- 1 star anise
- 1 tsp lemon zest
- 1 Tbsp erythritol

DIRECTIONS:
1. In a large saucepan, combine water, erythritol, cinnamon stick, cloves, star anise, and lemon zest and bring to a simmer.
2. Add the pears to the pan, ensure they are fully submerged, and simmer for about 20 minutes, or until pears are tender.
3. Remove pears and let them cool.
4. Reduce the liquid in the pan by half, until it forms a light syrup.
5. Serve the pears drizzled with the spiced syrup.

TIPS:
- Serve either warm or chilled, depending on preference.

- These poached pears can be stored in the refrigerator for up to 3 days.

NUTRITIONAL VALUES: Calories: 120, Fat: 0g, Carbs: 31g, Protein: 1g, Sugar: 20g, Glycemic Index (GI): Medium

Chocolate Avocado Mousse

PREPARATION TIME: 15 min

COOKING TIME: 0 min

MODE OF COOKING: Blending

INGREDIENTS:

- 2 ripe avocados, peeled and pitted
- 1/4 cup unsweetened cocoa powder
- 1/4 cup almond milk
- 2 Tbsp erythritol
- 1 tsp pure vanilla extract

DIRECTIONS:

1. Place all ingredients in a high-speed blender.
2. Blend on high until smooth and creamy.
3. Chill the mousse in the refrigerator for at least 30 minutes before serving.

TIPS:

- Top with a small handful of raspberries or a sprinkle of shredded coconut for added flavor and presentation.
- Ensure the mousse is well chilled; it enhances both the texture and taste.

NUTRITIONAL VALUES: Calories: 160, Fat: 12g, Carbs: 12g, Protein: 3g, Sugar: 1g, Glycemic Index (GI): Low

Lemon & Chia Seed Pudding

PREPARATION TIME: 10 min

COOKING TIME: 0 min (plus 4 hrs chilling)

MODE OF COOKING: Refrigerating

INGREDIENTS:

- 1/4 cup chia seeds
- 1 cup unsweetened almond milk

- 1 Tbsp erythritol
- 1 lemon, juiced and zested
- 1/2 tsp vanilla extract

DIRECTIONS:

1. In a bowl, combine almond milk, lemon juice and zest, erythritol, and vanilla extract.
2. Add chia seeds to the liquid and whisk thoroughly.
3. Let the mixture sit for about 10 minutes, then stir again to prevent clumping.
4. Cover and refrigerate for at least 4 hours or overnight until the pudding thickens.
5. Stir well before serving.

TIPS:

- If the pudding is too thick, add a little more almond milk to reach your desired consistency.
- Garnish with a few fresh berries for added flavor and color.

NUTRITIONAL VALUES: Calories: 90, Fat: 5g, Carbs: 8g, Protein: 3g, Sugar: 0g, Glycemic Index (GI): Low

2. FRUIT-BASED DELIGHTS

BERRY BLISS PARFAIT

PREPARATION TIME: 10 min

COOKING TIME: 0 min

MODE OF COOKING: Layering

INGREDIENTS:

- 1 cup Greek yogurt, plain and low-fat
- 1/2 cup blueberries
- 1/2 cup strawberries, sliced
- 2 Tbsp chia seeds
- 1 tsp pure vanilla extract
- Stevia to taste (optional)

DIRECTIONS:

1. In a small bowl, mix the Greek yogurt with vanilla extract and stevia to sweeten if desired.
2. Begin layering the parfaits by placing a portion of the yogurt mixture into the bottom of two glasses.
3. Follow with a layer of blueberries, then more yogurt, and a layer of sliced strawberries.
4. Sprinkle the top with chia seeds.
5. Repeat the layering if the glasses allow, or serve as is.

TIPS:

- Ensure the fruit is thoroughly washed and dried to maintain the parfait's freshness.
- The parfait can be refrigerated for up to an hour before serving to enhance the flavors.

NUTRITIONAL VALUES: Calories: 180, Fat: 4g, Carbs: 24g, Protein: 12g, Sugar: 15g, GI: Low

Citrus Mint Melon Balls

PREPARATION TIME: 15 min

COOKING TIME: 0 min

MODE OF COOKING: Chilling

INGREDIENTS:

- 1 cup watermelon, balled
- 1 cup cantaloupe, balled
- 1 cup honeydew melon, balled
- 2 Tbsp fresh mint leaves, chopped
- 1 lime, juiced
- 1/2 tsp lime zest

DIRECTIONS:

1. In a large bowl, combine the balled watermelon, cantaloupe, and honeydew.
2. In a small bowl, mix the lime juice and zest with chopped mint.
3. Drizzle the lime-mint mixture over the melon balls and gently toss to coat well.
4. Chill in the refrigerator for at least 30 minutes before serving to allow flavors to meld.

TIPS:

- Use a melon baller for uniform and visually appealing melon balls.
- Serve in a hollowed-out melon half for a decorative presentation.

NUTRITIONAL VALUES: Calories: 60, Fat: 0.5g, Carbs: 14g, Protein: 1g, Sugar: 12g, GI: Medium

NO-BAKE CHERRY DELIGHT

PREPARATION TIME: 20 min
COOKING TIME: 2 hr (chilling)
MODE OF COOKING: Chilling
INGREDIENTS:

- 2 cups pitted cherries, fresh or frozen
- 1 cup low-fat cream cheese
- 1/4 cup unsweetened almond milk
- 1 tsp pure vanilla extract
- Stevia to taste
- 1/4 cup crushed almonds for topping

DIRECTIONS:

1. In a blender, combine cherries, cream cheese, almond milk, vanilla extract, and stevia. Blend until smooth.
2. Pour the mixture into four small serving bowls.
3. Refrigerate for a minimum of 2 hours to set.
4. Before serving, garnish with crushed almonds.

TIPS:

- If using frozen cherries, ensure they are completely thawed to achieve a smooth texture in the cream blend.
- To enhance flavors, a dash of cinnamon can be blended into the mixture.

NUTRITIONAL VALUES: Calories: 150, Fat: 9g, Carbs: 13g, Protein: 6g, Sugar: 8g, GI: Low

PEAR GINGER CLUSTERS

PREPARATION TIME: 10 min

COOKING TIME: 0 min

MODE OF COOKING: Freezing

INGREDIENTS:

- 2 large pears, peeled and chopped
- 1/4 cup crystallized ginger, finely chopped
- 1 Tbsp lemon juice
- 1/2 cup water
- Stevia to taste

DIRECTIONS:

1. In a blender, combine pears, crystallized ginger, lemon juice, water, and stevia. Pulse until coarsely mixed.
2. Spoon the mixture into silicone molds or scoop onto a parchment-lined tray in small clusters.
3. Freeze until solid, about 4 hours.
4. Remove from molds or tray and serve immediately, or store in a freezer-safe container.

TIPS:

- Adjust the sweetness with more or less stevia depending on pear sweetness.
- Serve immediately after removing from the freezer for best texture.

NUTRITIONAL VALUES: Calories: 50, Fat: 0g, Carbs: 13g, Protein: 0g, Sugar: 10g, GI: Low

SNACKS AND SIDES

1. SAVORY SNACKS FOR STEADY BLOOD SUGAR

SMOKED SALMON AND AVOCADO ROLL-UPS

PREPARATION TIME: 15 min

COOKING TIME: 0 min

MODE OF COOKING: No cook

INGREDIENTS:

- 8 slices of smoked salmon
- 1 ripe avocado, thinly sliced
- 1/2 cucumber, julienned
- 4 Tbsp cream cheese, low-fat
- 1 Tbsp chopped dill
- 1 tsp lemon juice
- Salt and pepper to taste

DIRECTIONS:

1. Lay out the smoked salmon slices flat on a clean surface.
2. Spread each slice evenly with a thin layer of low-fat cream cheese.
3. On one edge of the salmon slice, arrange a few slices of avocado and a couple of julienned cucumber strips.
4. Sprinkle lemon juice, dill, salt, and pepper over the vegetables.
5. Carefully roll up the salmon around the filling, securing it with a toothpick if necessary.

6. Chill in the refrigerator for about 10 min before serving to set slightly.

TIPS:
- Ensure the avocado is ripe but firm to avoid mushiness in the roll-up.
- Serve with a light drizzle of extra virgin olive oil and a sprinkle of lemon zest for added flavor.

NUTRITIONAL VALUES: Calories: 140, Fat: 9g, Carbs: 4g, Protein: 12g, Sugar: 1g, Glycemic Index (GI): Low

CHICKPEA AND SPINACH STUFFED PORTOBELLOS

PREPARATION TIME: 15 min
COOKING TIME: 20 min
MODE OF COOKING: Baking
INGREDIENTS:
- 4 large portobello mushroom caps, stems removed
- 1 cup chickpeas, cooked
- 2 cups spinach, roughly chopped
- 1/2 cup feta cheese, crumbled
- 1/4 cup red onions, finely chopped
- 2 Tbsp olive oil
- 1 tsp minced garlic
- 1/2 tsp smoked paprika
- Salt and pepper to taste

DIRECTIONS:
1. Preheat the oven to 375°F (190°C).
2. In a skillet, heat 1 Tbsp of olive oil over medium heat. Add garlic and red onions, sautéing until translucent.
3. Add spinach to the skillet and cook until wilted. Remove from heat and let cool slightly.
4. In a bowl, mix together the cooked chickpeas, sautéed spinach and onions, feta cheese, and smoked paprika. Season with salt and pepper.
5. Brush the mushroom caps with the remaining olive oil and season with salt and pepper.

6. Stuff each mushroom cap with the chickpea and spinach mixture.
7. Bake in the preheated oven for 20 min, or until the mushrooms are tender and the filling is heated through.

TIPS:
- Serve hot with a drizzle of balsamic glaze for added sweetness and tang.
- These can be prepared ahead of time and baked just before serving for convenience.

NUTRITIONAL VALUES: Calories: 190, Fat: 10g, Carbs: 15g, Protein: 9g, Sugar: 2g, Glycemic Index (GI): Medium

2. GUILT-FREE SIDES FOR EVERY MEAL

Zesty Lemon Asparagus

PREPARATION TIME: 10 min

COOKING TIME: 15 min

MODE OF COOKING: Steaming

INGREDIENTS:

- 1 lb. fresh asparagus, trimmed
- 1 Tbsp extra-virgin olive oil
- 2 tsp lemon zest
- 2 Tbsp lemon juice
- 1/4 tsp salt
- 1/4 tsp black pepper
- 1 Tbsp chopped fresh parsley

DIRECTIONS:

1. Bring water to a boil in a steamer over high heat.
2. Place the asparagus in the steamer basket, cover, and steam until tender-crisp, about 7-10 minutes.
3. In a small bowl, mix together the olive oil, lemon zest, lemon juice, salt, and pepper.
4. Once asparagus is steamed, transfer it to a serving platter and drizzle with the lemon dressing.
5. Garnish with chopped parsley before serving.

TIPS:
- Choose asparagus stalks that are brightly colored and firm with tight, closed tips.
- Keep the dressed asparagus warm on a covered serving dish to preserve its tenderness.

NUTRITIONAL VALUES: Calories: 60, Fat: 3.6g, Carbs: 4g, Protein: 2.5g, Sugar: 2g, Glycemic Index (GI): Low

REFRESHING CUCUMBER-MINT SALAD

PREPARATION TIME: 15 min
COOKING TIME: 0 min
MODE OF COOKING: No Cooking
INGREDIENTS:
- 2 large cucumbers, thinly sliced
- 1/4 cup red onion, thinly sliced
- 1/4 cup fresh mint leaves, chopped
- 3 Tbsp apple cider vinegar
- 1 Tbsp extra-virgin olive oil
- Salt and pepper to taste

DIRECTIONS:
1. In a large bowl, combine the cucumber slices, red onion, and chopped mint.
2. Drizzle apple cider vinegar and olive oil over the mixture.
3. Season with salt and pepper to taste, and toss well to coat all the ingredients.
4. Chill in the refrigerator for about 10 minutes before serving to blend the flavors.

TIPS:
- Use a mandoline for uniformly thin cucumber slices.
- This salad is perfect as a refreshing side to grilled fish or chicken.

NUTRITIONAL VALUES: Calories: 50, Fat: 3.5g, Carbs: 4g, Protein: 1g, Sugar: 2g, Glycemic Index (GI): Low

Savory Roasted Green Beans

PREPARATION TIME: 10 min

COOKING TIME: 20 min

MODE OF COOKING: Roasting

INGREDIENTS:

- 1 lb. fresh green beans, ends trimmed
- 2 Tbsp extra-virgin olive oil
- 1 tsp garlic powder
- 1 tsp dried thyme
- Salt and pepper to taste

DIRECTIONS:

1. Preheat oven to 425°F (218°C).
2. In a large bowl, toss the green beans with olive oil, garlic powder, thyme, salt, and pepper.
3. Spread the beans in a single layer on a baking sheet.
4. Roast in preheated oven for 20 minutes, or until beans are tender and starting to brown.
5. Serve warm.

TIPS:

- Stir the beans halfway through roasting for even cooking.
- For a spicy kick, add a pinch of red pepper flakes before roasting.

NUTRITIONAL VALUES: Calories: 80, Fat: 5g, Carbs: 8g, Protein: 2g, Sugar: 4g, Glycemic Index (GI): Low

30 DAYS MEAL PLAN

DAY	Breakfast	Snack	Lunch	Snack	Dinner
DAY 1	Spinach and Feta Breakfast Scramble	Almond & Berry Breakfast Tart	Mediterranean Tuna and Bean Salad	Savory Roasted Green Beans	Diabetic-Friendly Stuffed Bell Peppers
DAY 2	Smoked Salmon and Avocado Salad	Cinnamon Spice Poached Pears	Spicy Shrimp and Avocado Salad	Zesty Lemon Asparagus	Lemon Herb Baked Salmon
DAY 3	Cauliflower Hash Browns	Chocolate Avocado Mousse	Zesty Lemon Herb Grilled Salmon	Refreshing Cucumber-Mint Salad	Creamy Tomato and Spinach Pasta
DAY 4	Greek Yogurt and Berry Parfait	Lemon & Chia Seed Pudding	Grilled Chicken Caesar Salad	Roasted Chickpeas	Zesty Lime and Herb Grilled Salmon
DAY 5	Tofu and Vegetable Stir-Fry	Berry Bliss Parfait	Quinoa and Veggie Bowl	Avocado Deviled Eggs	Mediterranean Stuffed Bell Peppers
DAY 6	Cinnamon Apple Chia Pudding	Citrus Mint Melon Balls	Turkey and Veggie Wrap	Mini Veggie Sticks with Hummus	Ginger Soy Tofu Stir-Fry
DAY 7	Berry Yoghurt Smoothie Bowl	No-Bake Cherry Delight	Asian Noodle Salad	Zucchini Chips	Grilled Chicken and Veggie Skewers
DAY 8	Fluffy Cottage Cheese Pancakes	Pear Ginger Clusters	Balsamic Chicken and Veggies	Cheese and Nut Platter	Baked Cod with Lemon and Garlic

DAY 9	Spinach and Mushroom Omelette	Smoked Salmon and Avocado Roll-Ups	Greek Chickpea Salad	Sugar-Free Energy Bites	Vegetarian Lentil Stew
DAY 10	Grapefruit and Avocado Salad	Chickpea and Spinach Stuffed Portobellos	Black Bean and Avocado Tacos	Cucumber Tuna Bites	Beef and Broccoli Stir-Fry
DAY 11	Spinach and Feta Breakfast Scramble	Almond & Berry Breakfast Tart	Mediterranean Tuna and Bean Salad	Savory Roasted Green Beans	Diabetic-Friendly Stuffed Bell Peppers
DAY 12	Smoked Salmon and Avocado Salad	Cinnamon Spice Poached Pears	Spicy Shrimp and Avocado Salad	Zesty Lemon Asparagus	Lemon Herb Baked Salmon
DAY 13	Cauliflower Hash Browns	Chocolate Avocado Mousse	Zesty Lemon Herb Grilled Salmon	Refreshing Cucumber-Mint Salad	Creamy Tomato and Spinach Pasta
DAY 14	Greek Yogurt and Berry Parfait	Lemon & Chia Seed Pudding	Grilled Chicken Caesar Salad	Roasted Chickpeas	Zesty Lime and Herb Grilled Salmon
DAY 15	Tofu and Vegetable Stir-Fry	Berry Bliss Parfait	Quinoa and Veggie Bowl	Avocado Deviled Eggs	Mediterranean Stuffed Bell Peppers
DAY 16	Cinnamon Apple Chia Pudding	Citrus Mint Melon Balls	Turkey and Veggie Wrap	Mini Veggie Sticks with Hummus	Ginger Soy Tofu Stir-Fry

DAY 17	Berry Yoghurt Smoothie Bowl	No-Bake Cherry Delight	Asian Noodle Salad	Zucchini Chips	Grilled Chicken and Veggie Skewers
DAY 18	Fluffy Cottage Cheese Pancakes	Pear Ginger Clusters	Balsamic Chicken and Veggies	Cheese and Nut Platter	Baked Cod with Lemon and Garlic
DAY 19	Spinach and Mushroom Omelette	Smoked Salmon and Avocado Roll-Ups	Greek Chickpea Salad	Sugar-Free Energy Bites	Vegetarian Lentil Stew
DAY 20	Grapefruit and Avocado Salad	Chickpea and Spinach Stuffed Portobellos	Black Bean and Avocado Tacos	Cucumber Tuna Bites	Beef and Broccoli Stir-Fry
DAY 21	Spinach and Feta Breakfast Scramble	Almond & Berry Breakfast Tart	Mediterranean Tuna and Bean Salad	Savory Roasted Green Beans	Diabetic-Friendly Stuffed Bell Peppers
DAY 22	Smoked Salmon and Avocado Salad	Cinnamon Spice Poached Pears	Spicy Shrimp and Avocado Salad	Zesty Lemon Asparagus	Lemon Herb Baked Salmon
DAY 23	Cauliflower Hash Browns	Chocolate Avocado Mousse	Zesty Lemon Herb Grilled Salmon	Refreshing Cucumber-Mint Salad	Creamy Tomato and Spinach Pasta
DAY 24	Greek Yogurt and Berry Parfait	Lemon & Chia Seed Pudding	Grilled Chicken Caesar Salad	Roasted Chickpeas	Zesty Lime and Herb Grilled Salmon

DAY 25	Tofu and Vegetable Stir-Fry	Berry Bliss Parfait	Quinoa and Veggie Bowl	Avocado Deviled Eggs	Mediterranean Stuffed Bell Peppers
DAY 26	Cinnamon Apple Chia Pudding	Citrus Mint Melon Balls	Turkey and Veggie Wrap	Mini Veggie Sticks with Hummus	Ginger Soy Tofu Stir-Fry
DAY 27	Berry Yoghurt Smoothie Bowl	No-Bake Cherry Delight	Asian Noodle Salad	Zucchini Chips	Grilled Chicken and Veggie Skewers
DAY 28	Fluffy Cottage Cheese Pancakes	Pear Ginger Clusters	Balsamic Chicken and Veggies	Cheese and Nut Platter	Baked Cod with Lemon and Garlic
DAY 29	Spinach and Mushroom Omelette	Smoked Salmon and Avocado Roll-Ups	Greek Chickpea Salad	Sugar-Free Energy Bites	Vegetarian Lentil Stew
DAY 30	Grapefruit and Avocado Salad	Chickpea and Spinach Stuffed Portobellos	Black Bean and Avocado Tacos	Cucumber Tuna Bites	Beef and Broccoli Stir-Fry

MEASUREMENT CONVERSION TABLE

Volume Conversions

Volume (Liquid)	US Customary Units	Metric Units
1 teaspoon	1 tsp	5 milliliters (ml)
1 tablespoon	1 tbsp	15 milliliters
1 fluid ounce	1 fl oz	30 milliliters
1 cup	1 cup	240 milliliters
1 pint	1 pt	473 milliliters
1 quart	1 qt	946 milliliters
1 gallon	1 gal	3.785 liters

Weight Conversions

Weight	US Customary Units	Metric Units
1 ounce	1 oz	28 grams (g)
1 pound	1 lb	454 grams
1 kilogram	2.2 lbs	1000 grams (1 kg)

Length Conversions

Length	US Customary Units	Metric Units
1 inch	1 in	2.54 centimeters (cm)
1 foot	1 ft	30.48 centimeters

Metric Volume Conversions

Volume	Metric Units	US Customary Units
1 milliliter (ml)	1 ml	0.034 fluid ounce (fl oz)
100 milliliters	100 ml	3.4 fluid ounces
1 liter (L)	1 L	34 fluid ounces
		4.2 cups
		2.1 pints
		1.06 quarts
		0.26 gallon

Metric Weight Conversions

Weight	Metric Units	US Customary Units
1 gram (g)	1 g	0.035 ounces (oz)
100 grams	100 g	3.5 ounces
500 grams	500 g	1.1 pounds (lb)
1 kilogram (kg)	1 kg	2.2 pounds

Temperature Conversions

Temperature	Celsius (°C)	Fahrenheit (°F)
Freezing Point	0°C	32°F
Refrigerator	4°C	39°F
Room Temperature	20°C - 22°C	68°F - 72°F
Boiling Water	100°C	212°F

CONCLUSION

As we come to a close in our journey through the *Diabetic Diet After 60 Cookbook*, I want to commend and thank you for your commitment and steadfast approach to managing diabetes through considered dietary changes. It's both a necessary adjustment and a substantial achievement. Reflecting on the topics we've covered, from understanding diabetes in older adults to adjusting your meal plans, what resonates the most is the underlying theme of empowerment. You've equipped yourself with knowledge, laid a foundation for healthier dining habits, and discovered that a diabetes-friendly diet can also be a doorway to delightful eating.

The road to managing diabetes at any age, particularly after 60, is not just about adhering to strict guidelines or feeling constrained by limitations. It's about re-envisioning life's latter years as a vibrant stage for implementing new, healthful practices that not only stabilize your blood sugar levels but also elevate your overall well-being. You have woven these new strategies into the fabric of daily living, showcasing your resilience and adaptability.

One critical takeaway I hope you've gathered from this book is the holistic approach to managing diabetes. We've tackled the importance of dietary adjustments, but alongside those, we've also emphasized the significance of lifestyle changes such as engaging in regular physical activity, maintaining social connections, and utilizing continuous learning and mental engagement to enrich both the mind and body. Each of these elements plays a symbiotic role in managing your diabetes effectively and joyfully. Adjusting to life's dietary rhythm changes naturally accompanies age, and integrating these smoothly can enhance your confidence in managing diabetes.

Moreover, navigating the nutritional landscape with diabetes doesn't require sacrificing the joys of delicious food. The recipes and meal planning guidelines offered in earlier chapters are aimed at proving that health-focused meals can also be heartwarming and palatable. Remember, creating a meal isn't just about mixing ingredients; it's an art of balancing flavors, nutrition, and blood sugar levels, all while weaving in personal taste and familial preferences.

In addressing diabetes, you've perhaps noticed that the challenge isn't solely about maintaining physical health but also about fostering a positive, proactive mindset. The stories and examples shared were selected not just for instruction but for resonance, designed to remind you that you are not alone on this path. Countless others are navigating similar challenges, and your journey could similarly inspire those around you. Sharing your story at family dinners or social gatherings can provide strength to others and build a supportive community around shared experiences and recipes.

Adapting to diabetic-friendly dietary habits also reflects broader themes of adaptation and acceptance, qualities that are invaluable as we age. Accepting diabetes as a part of your life's narrative can transform the management of this condition from a daily challenge into a testament of your life's wisdom and experience. Each meal planned, every snack prepared thoughtfully, is a reaffirmation of your dedication to living fully and healthily.

Looking forward to the continuity of your path, remember the importance of routine health checks with your medical professionals. Together with your dietary efforts, medical guidance is indispensable in adapting to how your body responds to treatments over time. Consider this book a companion in your culinary adventures, but let your healthcare provider be your guide in medical decisions.

As our narrative nears its end, I want to leave you with a call to embrace joy in every meal and encounter. Let the kitchen be a place of innovation and enjoyment. Invite family and friends to partake in your culinary creations. Laugh, share, and relish these moments, for each day presents an opportunity to craft something nutritiously delightful and heartening.

Lastly, remember, the journey of managing diabetes is continuous and evolving. What works today might need adjustment tomorrow. Stay curious, stay informed, and stay flexible to twist and turn along with life's changes. You have the tools, you have the knowledge, and now, you have the culinary prowess to maintain an enjoyable, diabetes-friendly lifestyle.

Thank you for allowing me to be a part of your journey. Let the chapters of this book serve not just as a memory to revisit but as a timeless guide as you continue to navigate the beautiful complexity of life with diabetes beyond 60. Here's to many more years of health, happiness, and hearty meals. Cheers to your continued success and vitality.

THANK YOU FROM THE BOTTOM OF MY HEART

Dear Reader,

A big thank you for selecting my book! I truly hope you find as much joy in reading it as I did in writing it. Your support means the world to me and is deeply valued.

When you have a moment, please consider leaving a review. Your honest thoughts not only aid in my growth as an author but also guide other readers in their choices.

To show my gratitude, I invite you to scan the QR code below for a special bonus gift exclusive to you.

Thank you once more for being a part of this journey.

Warmest regards,

Jonny Bakers

Made in the USA
Columbia, SC
18 March 2025